DENIM
by design

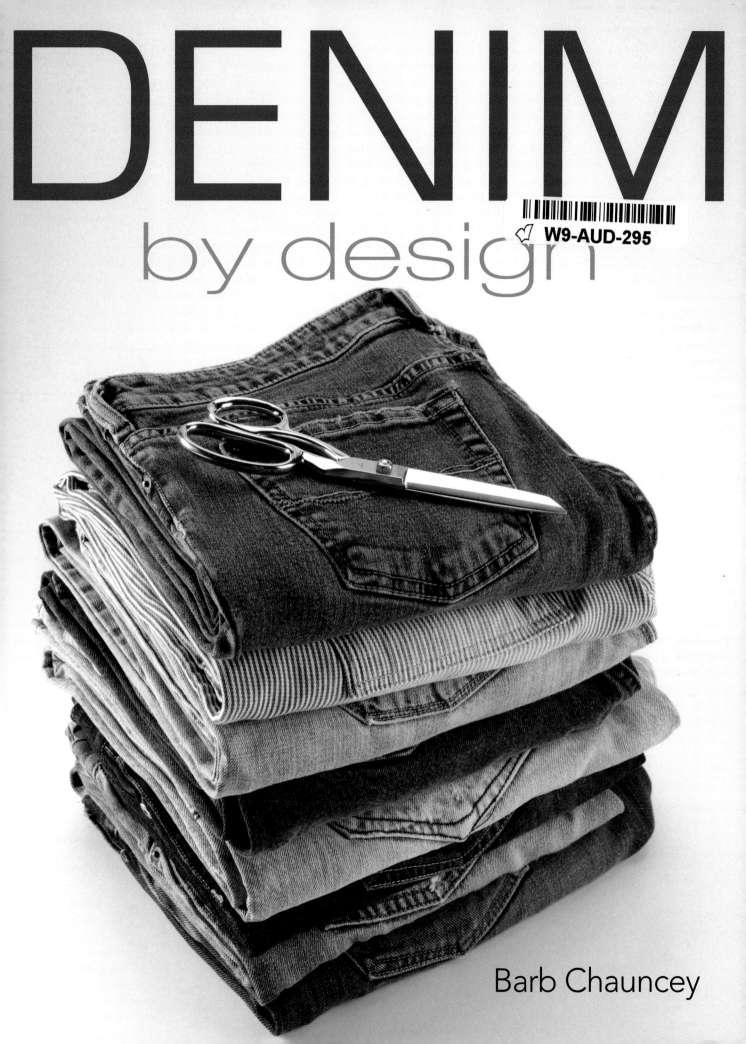

Barb Chauncey

Published by

700 East State Street • Iola, WI 54990-0001
715-445-2214 • 888-457-2873
www.krausebooks.com

Our toll-free number to place an order or obtain
a free catalog is (800) 258-0929.

The following registered trademark terms and companies appear in this
book: X-ACTO, Dritz Jean-a-ma-jig, Teflon, BeDazzler, Levi Strauss,
Gitano, Bugle Boy, Faded Glory, G.H. Bass, American Outpost, Lee,
Z Cavaricci, Place Jeanswear, Wrangler, Tommy Hilfiger, Dickies.

Library of Congress Control Number: 2007924851

ISBN-13: 978-0-89689-598-0
ISBN-10: 0-89689-598-X

Designed by Donna Mummery
Edited by Andy Belmas

Printed in the United States of America

Contents

Accessories 96

Resources 126

Getting Started

Welcome to the world of fashion design, customized to your size and taste! This book will show you how to make vests, purses, belts and other accessories all from cast-off jeans. Each item is embellished, giving you many options for fashion expression.

You could purchase denim fabric for the designs if you wish, or use some of your favorite jeans that no longer fit. Garage sales and second hand shops are also a great source of jeans. Many of the embellishments can be added to purchased vests if that works better for you.

Here are a few tips for selecting denim. For vests, try to find a couple pairs of jeans in the same color and weight. Larger jeans will have areas big enough for some of the vest back and front pieces. Usually the largest area is found in the back below the pockets. Very stiff denim is harder to work with, especially if there are lots of curved seams in the project.

Stretch denim usually ravels easier, so select a seam finish such as the flat felled seam when working with it.

Try to store the denim flat and as wrinkle free as possible. Set in wrinkles are sometimes difficult to work with.

Look for jeans with unique yokes or other features, such as inside pockets. These can be used to dress up a vest or purse.

The jean jumper is a tool that can be used to assist in stitching over seams or when hemming over a seam that is very bulky. It is a small piece of plastic that holds the presser foot of the machine up slightly, allowing it to stitch through the bulky area. An example of this tool is the Dritz Jean-a-ma-jig.

A sharp, heavier needle in the sewing machine also helps with bulky areas. Jeans or denim needles are specially designed to pierce denim fabric.

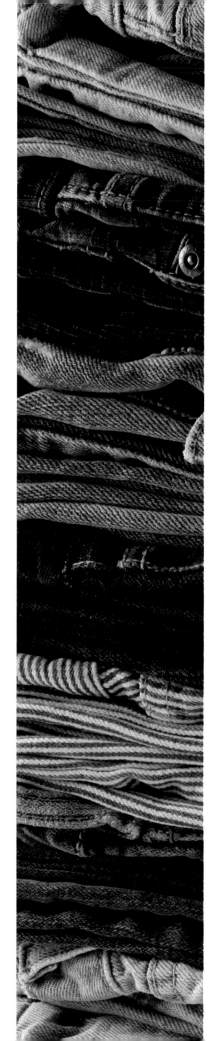

Customizing the Pattern

Begin by measuring on your model's body to see if you need to adjust the pattern for fit. This diagram shows various places to check measurements. The first measurement checks the length from the back of your neck to the bottom of the vest, including the hem. The second measurement is from one underarm to the other across the back. Most pattern pieces for the back have two pieces, so calculate the finished width by measuring between seam allowances. Measurement five plus seven would be your measurement at the hemline. Be sure to allow for some overlap if the vest has an overlapping closure. Continue with other measurements as suggested in the diagram.

After you have taken some measurements and made any major adjustments, it is best to find some inexpensive fabric, which can be from another garment, to test the fit of the pattern. Cut and use a long stitch to sew the main pattern pieces to see if you need to adjust the size to fit you. You may want to stitch the seams with wrong sides together, leaving the seams on the outside so they are easier to pin to adjust the size. You may need to cut the piece and add more fabric if it is too small. When you are satisfied with the fit, rip the seams apart and use the cloth as the pattern.

> **tip**
> The seam allowance is ½". The thickness of the denim may determine if you can turn the neck edge over just ½" or slightly more to get the raw edge folded under.

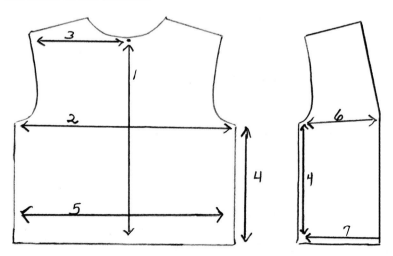

Sewing Terms

A **layered seam** is a seam where the seam allowance is trimmed shorter on one piece of fabric than on the other to reduce bulk. Generally, the seam allowance that is closest to the body is trimmed closer to the seam, unless instructed otherwise.

A **clipped seam** is a seam with triangle shaped wedges cut from the seam allowance. Usually a clipped seam is made on curved areas so the seam will lay flat when the garment is turned right-side-out. When cutting, do not clip through the seam.

A **flat felled seam** is a seam finish common on denim clothing. The fabric is laid wrong sides together and the seam is stitched. One seam allowance is trimmed close to the seam. The other seam allowance is folded, laid over the trimmed seam allowance, and stitched down.

A **reverse flat felled seam** is made in the same way, but starting with the right sides of the fabric together.

Stitch-in-the-ditch is a method of understitching where you stitch very near the seam or in the seam itself. This technique holds the fabric in place and hides the stitching.

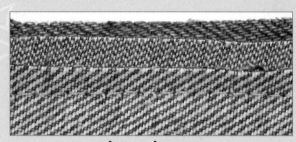

layered seam

clipped seam

flat felled seam

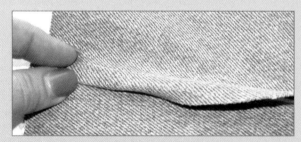

reverse flat felled seam

stitch-in-the-ditch

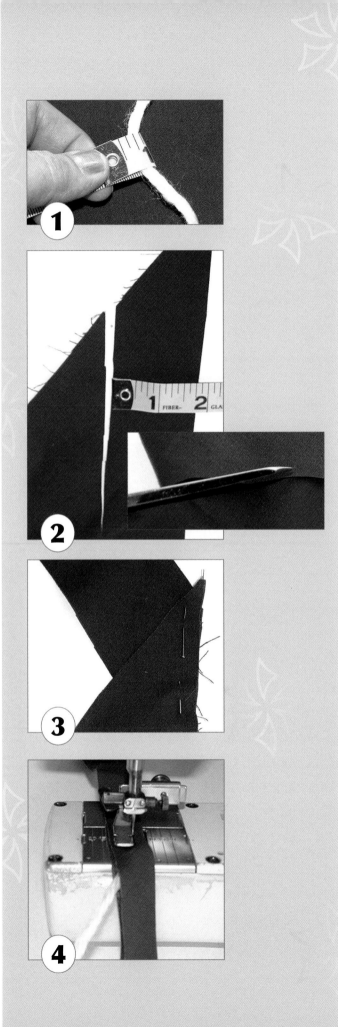

Making Bias Tape

1 Using a tape measure, measure around the cording to see how wide the fabric needs to be to cover the cording. Don't forget to leave a seam allowance on each side.

2 Make one cut along the bias of the fabric (forty-five degree angle to straight grain of fabric). Measure from the edge and cut the bias strips. It is easy to keep cutting the same width if you fold the strip you have cut over onto the fabric and use it for a guide.

3 If you need a bias strip longer than the fabric you have cut, join two bias strips. To join bias strips, lay the pieces with right sides together as shown and stitch. Press the seam open. Be sure the seam allowance is on the inside when stitching the fabric around the cord.

4 To complete the bias tape, attach a zipper foot to your sewing machine. Wrap the bias strip around the cord. Keep the seam allowance even and stitch close to the cord.

Vests

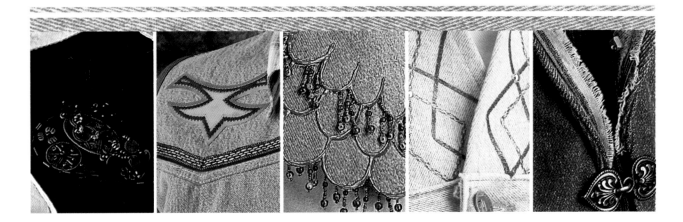

Sparkles Vest

You don't have to sew a vest to dress it up. Here is a purchased vest that's very easy to embellish. The rhinestones really sparkle on the dark denim.

Difficulty Level: Very Easy

Materials

* Denim vest
* Two sets of two iron-on fashion designs
* Hot-fix crystals (3 mm)
* Rhinestone trim
* Scissors
* Rhinestone applicator
* Needle
* Gray thread

1 Follow the manufacturer's instructions to apply an iron-on fashion design to each pocket. Cut apart the other two iron-on fashion designs and apply part to the lower front and part to the point of the collar on each side.

2 Follow the manufacturer's instructions to apply the rhinestones to the front of the vest and to the edge of the pocket as shown.

3 Cut white rhinestone trim to fit along the vest front under the pockets and on the yoke. Use needle and thread to hand stitch the trim to the vest. Cut trim to fit along the back yoke and hand stitch in place.

4 Use seam sealant on ends of trim to prevent fraying.

Sparkles Vest   **15**

Lacy Vest

Here is a girly looking vest that is quick to make. You may wish to use contrasting thread for top stitching and for the flat felled seams. The fit of this vest can easily be adjusted because the flat felled seams are first stitched with right sides of the fabric together. The appliqué trim is already made—just add the beaded trim.

Difficulty Level:
Easy

Materials
❋ Denim

❋ Two ready-made lacy appliqués (approx. 6" wide)

❋ 18" beaded trim

❋ 2⅔ yd. flat white lace (1¼" wide)

❋ Fabric paint (optional) in white, buttermilk, burnt sienna, pink, blue or to match appliqué

❋ Seam sealant

❋ Scissors

❋ Sewing machine and thread

❋ Foam brush

❋ Paint palette

❋ Plastic lid

❋ Freezer paper

❋ Cardboard

❋ Water container

1 Use the enclosed pattern to cut the front and back pieces for the vest. Stitch the back, side, and shoulder seams with the wrong sides of the fabric together. Try on to check fit. Stitch darts if needed.

2 Trim one seam allowance to ¼". Fold the other seam allowance and top stitch it over the top of the trimmed allowance to make a flat felled seam finish. Use seam sealant on all raw edges and allow to dry.

3 I chose to paint the flat lace so it would match my appliqué. To paint the lace, cover a piece of cardboard with freezer paper, waxy side up. Lay out lace on paper one section at a time. Put paint on a palette. Dip brush in a little water then dip into white paint. Add a little cream, burnt sienna, and pink and daub on the palette to mix the paint in the brush. Adjust the color by adding more paint until it resembles the background color of the appliqué. Apply to lace, leaving some spaces to put blue paint as in the appliqué. Continue until all lace is painted. Allow to dry.

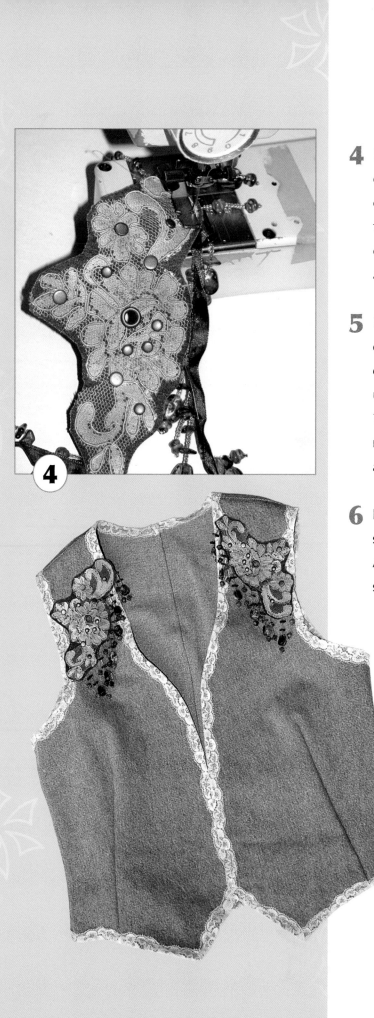

4 Use a zipper foot to stitch ribbon edge of beaded trim behind the lower edge of the appliqué so the beads dangle from the bottom. Make sure the ribbon does not show below the edge of the appliqué.

5 Fold lace in half lengthwise and place over raw edge of vest, starting at back of neck. Stitch lace to entire vest edge using a zigzag stitch. Fold lace under ¼" at end to finish. Sew lace in same manner to armhole openings, beginning at bottom of armhole.

6 Pin appliqué pieces in place and use a straight stitch to stitch them to the vest. A zipper foot may be used to help avoid studs on the appliqué pieces.

Pant Leg Vest

Do you have a favorite pair of jeans with a nice border? Turn those jeans into this vest! Or you could add this border to a plain pair of jeans for a great look. The design is easy, as some seams are already sewn for you.

Difficulty Level: Easy

Materials

❋ Jeans

❋ Two jeans pockets

❋ Iron-on trim (wildflower motif)

❋ 50" length of 1" braid

❋ Two buttons

❋ Rhinestone studs

❋ Stud setting tool

❋ Glitter paint in green, yellow, purple, pink

❋ Seam ripper

❋ Scissors

❋ Sewing machine

❋ Needle and thread

❋ Cardboard

1 Use seam ripper to open the non-flat felled seams on both jeans legs. Place pattern on opened jean surface.

2 Open bottom of hem 3" on each side of lower center back sections. With right sides together, stitch entire back seam, then stitch hem closed again. Pin seam at shoulder to check fit and adjust size of arm hole if necessary.

3 Follow manufacturer's instructions to apply iron-on trim to both sides of the front of the vest about 1" from hem. You may also add iron-on trim to the back of the vest. Lay trim just above original hem and topstitch in place all the way around.

4 Cut out two pockets. Cut away the fabric from the back of the pockets. Lay the pocket over the front of the vest at the shoulder seam. Trim edges of pocket to fit vest. Stitch trim to the front of the pocket through all thicknesses so the pocket attaches to the vest. Repeat for both sides of the vest.

5 Stitch shoulder seams with wrong sides together and finish with flat felled seams.

6 To make bias trim, cut diagonal strips 2" wide with diagonal cuts on all ends. Stitch several strips together by matching ends, right sides together and stitching to form one long piece.

7 Cut end of bias strip off straight and fold under ¼". Lay right sides together on outside of vest and stitch all around front opening. Clip curves. Fold bias strip over and turn raw edge under to make ½" wide. Pin baste. Stitch-in-the-ditch on the right side to close the bias edge. Follow same procedure to finish armholes.

8 Fold tab piece, right sides together, and stitch leaving it open between dots. Trim corners and point close to stitching. Turn right-side-out. Fold seam to inside at opening and topstitch around tab close to edge. Attach to vest using buttons. This may be used to gather fabric at back of vest for a closer fit.

9 Use stud setting tool to add rhinestone studs to front.

10 Put cardboard piece behind iron-on trim area and use glitter fabric paint to fill in leaves and flowers as desired. Let dry according to manufacturer's directions.

tip
Thinner denim is easier to work with for edge trim.

Difficulty Level:
Easy

Materials
❋ Denim

❋ Striped ribbon trim

❋ 2" Deco discs
  (turquoise)

❋ Yellow topstitching
  thread

❋ Seam sealant

❋ Scissors

❋ Sewing machine

❋ Pins

Rings Vest

Here is a vest with clean lines and great design elements. It is really simple to construct and goes together quickly.

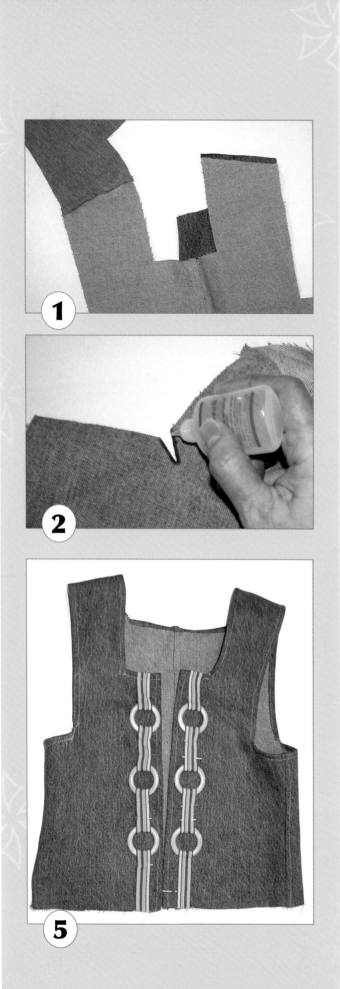

1 Use the enclosed pattern sheets to cut the pattern pieces from the denim. Stitch the back seam, side seams, and shoulder seams. Check fit. Use yellow thread and a flat felled seam to finish the seams.

2 Fold the front edge over twice to hide the raw edge. Top stitch as before using yellow thread.

3 Clip square corners of neck and armhole areas. Apply seam sealant to clip so it won't ravel. Allow to dry.

4 Turn edges under, as in step 2, to finish armhole areas.

5 Mark trim and ring placement on the front of the vest. Cut the trim pieces with ¾" extra on each end to hold rings. Pin trim and rings in place. Stitch sides of trim in matching thread. Wrap ends of trim around rings and straight stitch to hold rings in place.

6 Fold edges at neck area, as in step two, and top stitch to finish the neck. Finish the lower edge in the same way.

Difficulty Level:
Moderate

Materials
❊ Denim

❊ Iron-on silver ribbon
(1/8")

❊ Mini-iron to apply
trim

❊ 32" length of
beaded fringe

❊ 32" length of sequin
flower trim

❊ Seam sealant

❊ Scissors

❊ Sewing machine

❊ Pins

❊ Fabric glue

❊ Fabric hot glue or
needle and thread

Beaded
Fringe Vest

Go all out with beads and trims on this
great vest. Layering the trims gives a really
finished look.

1 Cut pattern pieces from denim. Stitch back seam, side seams, and shoulder seams. Check fit. To finish seams, trim one seam allowance to ¼" and fold the other over it to hide raw edges. Top stitch to hold folded edge in place.

2 Fold front edge over twice to hide raw edge. Top stitch as in step one.

3 Clip square corners of neck and armhole areas. Apply seam sealant to clipped areas so they won't ravel. Allow to dry.

4 Turn edges under, as in step two, to finish armhole, front, and neck areas.

5 Finish neck and front edges by turning under twice and stitching. Make sure the distance from the neckline to the hemline is the same length on both sides. Follow manufacturer's directions for mini-iron to apply iron-on ribbon around neck and front.

6 Mark trim placement on front of vest. Cut beaded fringe with a little extra at each end. To keep fringe from fraying, cut end bead from last strand on each end. Pull beads off leaving thread. Catch that thread in stitching when sewing the ribbon along the top of the beaded fringe.

7 Use fabric glue to attach sequin trim over ribbon at top of beaded fringe. Allow to dry.

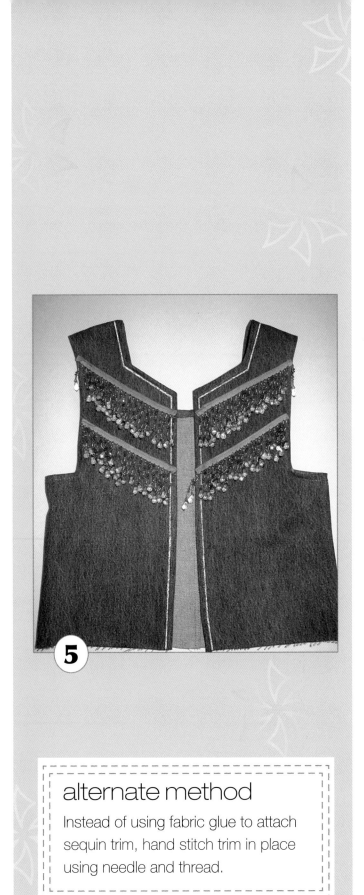

alternate method

Instead of using fabric glue to attach sequin trim, hand stitch trim in place using needle and thread.

Black Vest

Here is a fun, classy vest that goes together quickly with only a few sewing challenges. Since the seams are flat felled, some are rather thick to stitch over when hemming. A jean jumper really helps with that. The rhinestones can even be stitched onto the vest if your machine has a hem stitch.

Difficulty Level: Moderate

Materials
* 2 pair black jeans

* 1²/₃ yd. black hairy gimp

* 2 yd. black rhinestone trim

* 2 denim patches or appliqués

* 2⁷/₈" clasp

* Scissors

* Sewing machine

* Thread

* Jean jumper

* Pins

* Needle

1 Cut out pattern pieces and stitch all seams, except facing, wrong sides together. Try on to check fit and adjust if necessary. Use a flat felled seam to finish all seams.

2 Stitch center seam of facing. Turn outside edge of facing under ¼" and zigzag to finish. Lay facing over front opening of vest, right sides together, matching center back seams. Stitch, stopping ½" from bottom edge of facing. Trim seam allowance in graduated layers. Clip curves.

3 Clip vest seam allowance at end of facing stitching. This will allow you to turn the rest of the hem edge under, hiding raw edge. Topstitch hem. Use a jean jumper to help go over bulky seams.

4 Finish armhole edges by turning under twice and stitching.

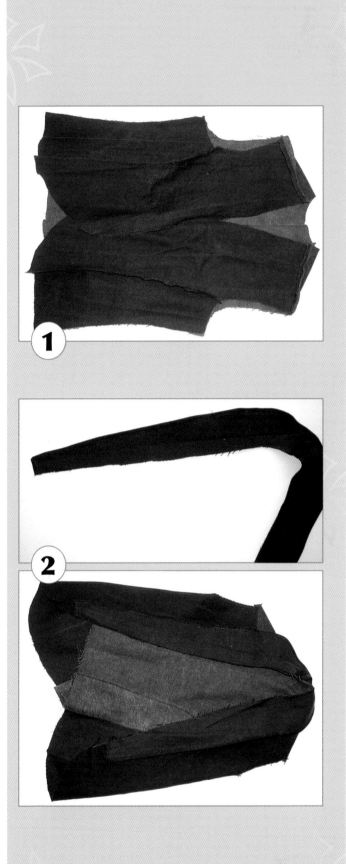

5 To attach trim, turn end of braid under ³/₈". Place trim on right side of vest, beginning at end of facing. Stitch to opposite end of facing and finish end of trim by folding under ³/₈".

6 Position rhinestone trim along hemline, beginning at side front seam. Rhinestone trim should lay over top of first trim, about ³/₈" from edge of vest. Use a hemstitch with the appropriate foot and stitch length so that the stitch penetrates the trim between each rhinestone.

7 Position appliqué hearts in place at shoulder and stitch to vest, using your stitch of choice.

8 Hand stitch clasp just below first trim at center front of vest.

Men's Vest

Hey guys, we're not leaving you out! Here's a vest for you. Pick out your favorite trim to accent the denim. The iron-on patch makes embellishing easy. The wide trim needs to be cut in half for some parts of this vest. You could substitute 1" trim for those areas for easier application of the trim.

Difficulty Level:
Moderate

Materials

✴ Two pairs of matching jeans

✴ 2½ yd. woven trim (2¼" wide) Note: could substitute 5 yd. of 1" braid

✴ Coordinating, double-fold bias tape (½" folded width)

✴ Two bird-themed iron-on patches

✴ Yellow top stitching thread for jeans

✴ Scissors

✴ Sewing machine

✴ Thread

✴ Iron

✴ Press cloth

1 Cut out all pieces. Stitch seams in this order: Back seams, front seams, front yoke seams, side seams, shoulder seams. Leave back yoke seam until later. Finish seams as inside flat felled seams with double top stitching in yellow jeans thread. Then stitch back yoke to back and finish seam in a similar manner.

2 If using wide trim, it can be cut in half lengthwise. Before cutting, narrowly zigzag on both sides of center line to keep cut edges from unraveling. Cut a piece of trim the correct length to fit along top of front yoke, adding extra to turn under at ends. Turn under ¼" on ends of trim and stitch trim in place.

3 Decide if you want the back trim to be straight or V-shaped. Cut a piece of trim the necessary length and fold to form a V, beginning at center back. Turn under ¼" at ends of trim and stitch.

tip
Check vest measurements before cutting trim to designated lengths.

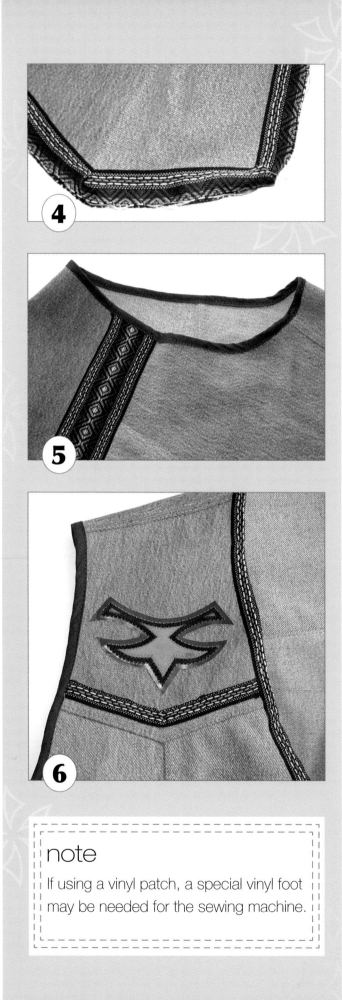

4 Wide trim can be cut in half lengthwise as in step two. Splice ends to make one long piece. Starting at center back, place outer edge of trim so that it extends ½" beyond vest edge. Stitch trim in place, making tucks or pleats at corners to allow trim to lay flat. Turn end of trim under when you reach the end and stitch in place, overlapping starting point. Turn vest to inside, fold trim over raw edge and stitch to vest.

5 Place purchased bias tape over raw edge of fabric, beginning at base of armhole. Stitch around armhole, folding end under and overlapping starting point.

6 Follow manufacturers instructions to attach patch to center of vest front yoke.

note

If using a vinyl patch, a special vinyl foot may be needed for the sewing machine.

Scalloped Vest

This vest features a unique use of fabric paint and fabric hot glue, which is used to add beaded trim. The colors could be changed to match something special in your wardrobe. This vest is a little more fragile and would need to be hand washed in cold water. Handle it gently and hang to dry.

Difficulty Level: Moderate

Materials
* Denim
* Pink fabric paint
* Paint applicator (optional)
* 1⅞ yd. beaded trim
* Scissors
* Cardboard cut to size of pattern pieces
* Pins
* Sewing machine
* Thread
* Hot glue gun
* Tracing paper

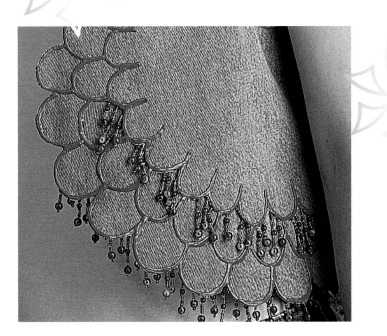

1 Cut out pattern pieces. Stitch center back seam and finish with inside flat felled seam finish. Use tracing paper to transfer scallop pattern to fabric. Pin fabric to cardboard. Follow manufacturer's instructions to apply paint to all scallop lines. Allow to dry thoroughly.

2 Cut excess fabric outside scallops at hem edge. Stitch side seams and shoulder seams with an inside flat felled seam finish. Turn back neck edge under twice and top stitch to finish neck. Use same method to finish armhole edges.

3 To finish end of beaded trim, fold end of ribbon under and glue. Glue trim between dots according to markings on pattern.

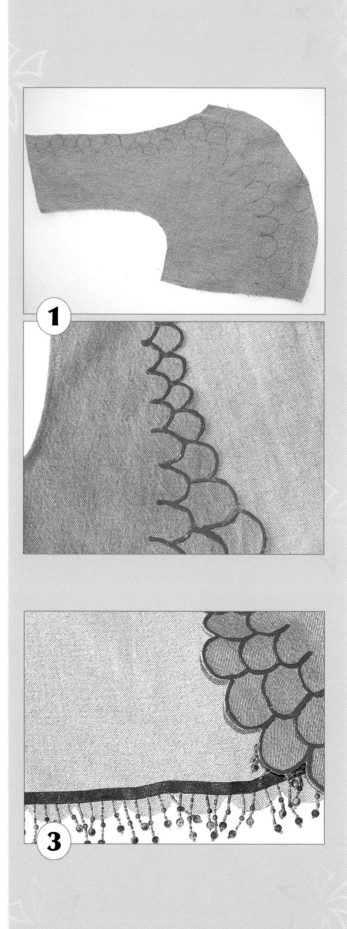

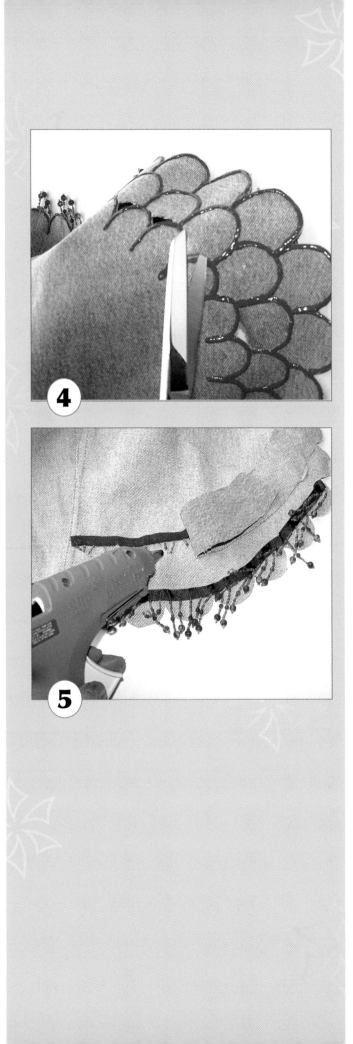

4 Cut slits below each top row scallop to create openings for beads to come through. Be careful not to cut through the paint; only between scallops. Place beaded trim on wrong side of vest and work beads through the openings to the vest front.

5 Smooth cut fabric areas back into place. Using hot glue, glue ribbon from beaded trim onto back of vest. Use additional fabric and glue to cover any remaining fabric slits.

Diamond Vest

Want to use a fancy yoke from a favorite pair of jeans? Turn it into this vest, then embellish it to suit your own style and color scheme. Before beginning, be sure there is enough yoke to fit around your waist.

Difficulty Level: Experienced

Materials:

* ❋ Jeans with yoke top all the way around
* ❋ Iron-on ribbon; one spool blue, one spool blue and red
* ❋ 22 metal studs
* ❋ Scissors
* ❋ Pins
* ❋ Thread
* ❋ Seam ripper
* ❋ Iron and Teflon pressing sheet
* ❋ Stud setting tool

1 Cut yoke from jeans, making sure it fits around waist as this will be the bottom of the vest. If front and back yoke of jeans do not meet, leave fabric below waistband and hem raw edge with double stitching.

Make basic pattern for back and front as shown in diagram.

Measurement 1 = back of neck to waist;

2 = under arm to under arm;

3 = center back to shoulder edge of vest;

4 = under arm to waist;

5 = waist back;

6 = under arm to center front;

7 = waist side to center front;

Note: Measurements 5 + 7 must equal length of waistband.

2 Cut back from denim, stitch center seam, and finish with flat felled seam. Cut both front pieces.

3 Cut fabric at base of zipper area ¼" below yoke line. Trim corners ¼" and turn raw edge to inside. Stitch closed. Cut away excess zipper fabric as close to seam as possible.

4 Stitch shoulder and side seams of vest. Try on to assure fit and adjust if necessary. Use flat felled seam finish. Finish center front edge by turning raw edge under twice and stitching ¼" from edge.

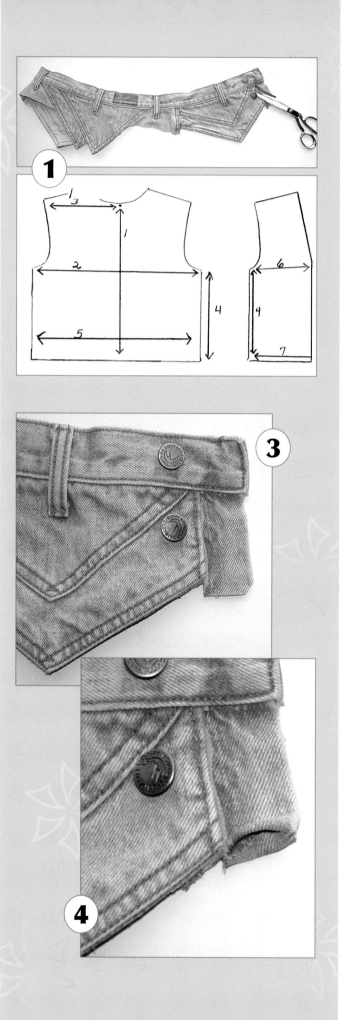

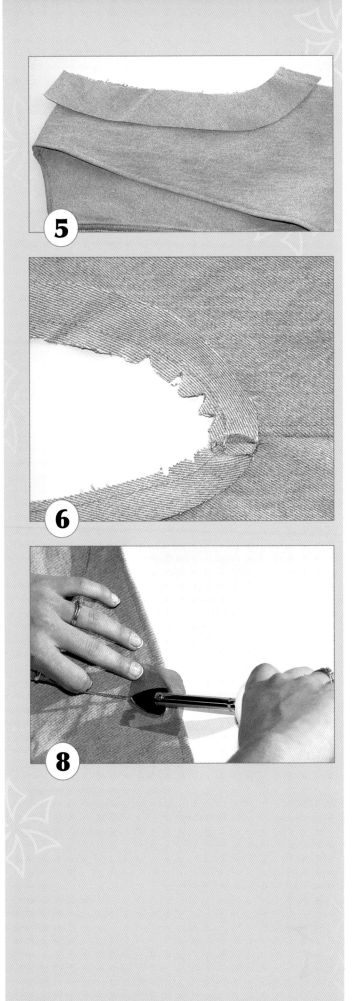

5 Cut narrow facing or 1½"-1¾" wide bias to fit armholes as shown in photo. Join front and back armhole facing, right sides together and stitch. Pin baste facing over armhole, right sides together, and stitch in place.

6 Clip armhole seam at curves. Fold facing to inside, turning raw edge under once. If finished width of facing will be more than ½", unfold and trim so it will be only ½" when folded under. Stitch in place using double stitching.

7 Clip open top of waistband above yoke. Insert body of vest ½" into waistband and stitch closed.

8 Mark diamond pattern onto vest body by inserting pins at side points of each diamond. Adjust pattern around curves of neck as needed, making sure the diamond pattern matches on both sides of the vest. Heat iron. Beginning at waistband, place iron-on ribbon, following pattern. Cover with small piece of Teflon sheet and iron to adhere. Continue to cover diamond pattern with ribbon until design is completed.

9 Attach studs following manufacturer's instructions.

Shawl Collar Vest

The style of this vest is the same as the Black Vest, except it has a shawl collar instead of trim around the neck, and the front sections are lined instead of faced. If you would rather use a facing, the facing pattern from the Black Vest may be used. If you use denim for a facing it will add more thickness; a thin lining works well even though it is a bit more work.

Difficulty Level:
Experienced

Materials
* Two or three pair of jeans
* 2 yd. beaded denim trim
* 2" clasp
* Scissors
* Sewing machine
* Thread
* Jean jumper
* Pins
* Needle

1 Cut out all pattern pieces and stitch all seams, except upper collar and under collar, wrong sides together. Finish all seams with flat felled finish. Turn hem edge of back vest section under twice and top stitch; the back will not be lined.

2 Stitch center seams of both upper and under collars. Lay upper and under collar right sides together and stitch outer edge.

3 Cut pocket from jeans and remove any excess fabric inside pocket. Place trim across top of pocket, tucking ends behind pocket to hide. Stitch trim to pocket. Place pocket on vest and top stitch in place. Repeat for other side of vest.

4 With right sides together and matching center back seams, stitch under collar section only to vest from shoulder seam to shoulder seam, being sure not to catch upper collar in stitching. Clip through all layers at end of stitching. Layer seam allowances and clip curves.

5 Stitch both layers of remaining under and upper collar sections to vest front on both sides.

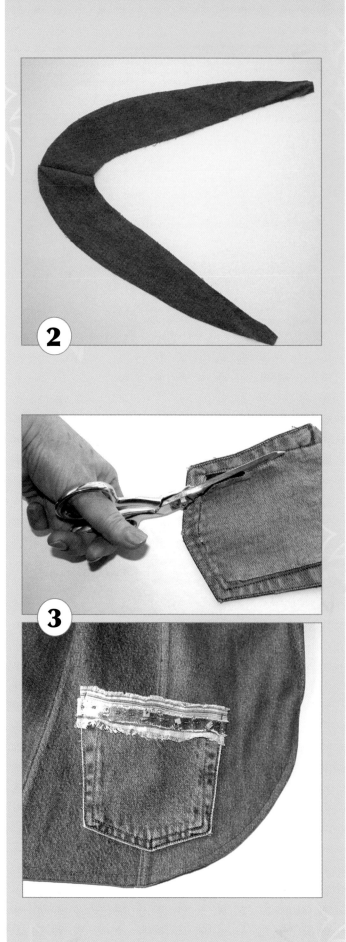

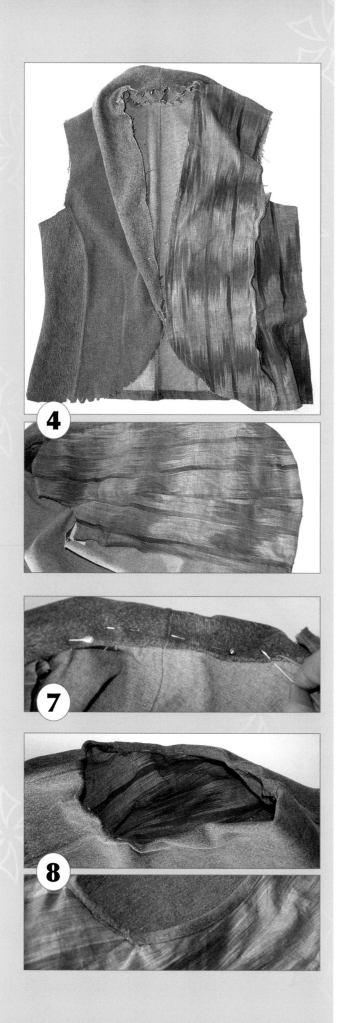

6 Stitch center seams of front lining and zigzag seam allowances to finish. Lay lining sections over vest fronts, right sides together. Stitch from front shoulder down entire vest front, stitching through vest, collar, and lining. Turn lining to inside of vest. Fold raw edges of lining under at shoulder and side seams and stitch from right side of vest, following stitching lines on flat felled seams to secure lining.

7 Turn seam allowance of upper collar under between shoulder seams and hand stitch closed.

8 Turn armhole edges under twice and pin. Topstitch ¼" from edge.

9 To attach trim to collar, fold one end of trim under ¼" and stitch to keep from fraying. Lay trim on collar with finished end of trim extending past end of collar 2". Pin baste trim to collar all around to other end of collar. Cut trim 2¼" past end of collar. Fold trim under and stitch at first end to keep trim from fraying. Stitch trim to collar. Hand stitch ends of trim to inside of vest.

10 Use needle and thread to stitch clasp to front of vest.

Bags

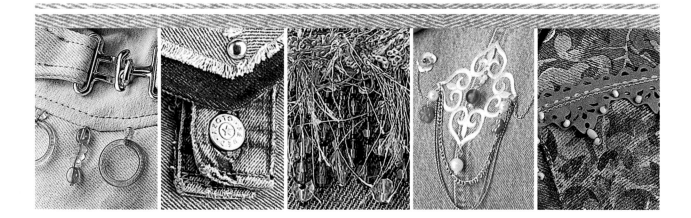

Clutch Purse

Wear it with a chain or carry it like a clutch purse, either way this little bag grabs the glitz. Little beads form a frosty edging around the flap and on the back of the bag. Choose your favorite long, narrow bead for a closure.

Difficulty Level: Easy

Materials
* Denim
* Twelve belt loops
* Silver glitter fabric paint
* Assorted small glass beads (clear and silver)
* Fabric glue or hot glue
* Three silver grommets
* Bead approx. 5/8" to fit through closure grommet
* Two silver snap rings
* Lightweight chain (40" or length desired)
* Elastic thread to attach bead
* Scissors
* Sewing machine
* Needle
* Hammer
* Pins
* Cardboard
* Hot glue gun (optional)

1 Use pattern to cut purse, sides, and lining from denim.

2 Lay purse side pieces onto main purse section, right sides together, matching dots one and two. Stitch between dots. Clip seam allowance through all layers to dots. Pivot side pieces and match to main purse section. Stitch to dots three and four.

3 Clip corners and layer seam. Turn side seam allowances toward main purse section and topstitch on right side, 1/8" away from seam line.

4 Repeat above steps to assemble lining. With purse wrong-side-out and lining right-side-out, push lining into purse. Stitch around purse and lining, leaving entire front seam open to turn it right-side-out.

5 Clip curves on purse flap. Trim seams so the curves will lay flat when turned right-side-out.

6 Turn purse right-side-out. Clip seam allowances at sides of front opening. Turn seam allowances of opening to the inside and topstitch to close opening. Begin topstitching along top edge of purse side, around the flap and then along the other top edge of the other purse side.

note

If you wish to use other fabric for lining, put iron-on interfacing on back of denim for added body.

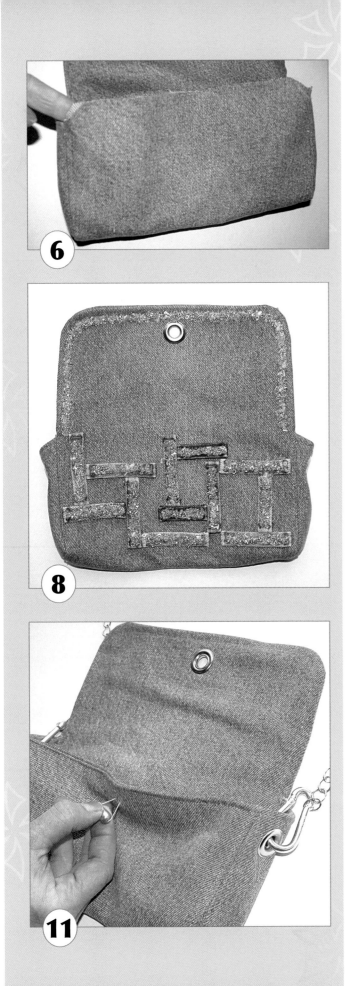

7 Follow manufacturer's instructions to install grommets. Place one in center front of flap, with center of grommet 1" from edge of purse. Place one grommet centered on each purse side with center of grommet ¾" from edge.

8 Arrange belt loops on purse back, choosing various sizes to make desired pattern. Remove belt loops from purse. Squeeze glitter paint on top of each belt loop and pour glass beads over paint, gently pressing beads into paint. Allow to dry.

9 Use pins to hold purse on cardboard. Squeeze a heavy line of glitter paint just inside top stitching line of purse flap. Pour glass beads on wet paint and allow to dry.

10 Use fabric glue to attach belt loops to back of purse. Allow to dry.

11 Put chain onto snap rings, being careful not to twist chain. Attach snap rings to grommets on each purse side.

12 Use elastic thread to stitch bead to purse center front.

Daisy Tote

Here's a fun tote that is easy to construct and fun to paint. I used an air-powered fabric painter to add the paint. It helps make the tiny lines and great details. Beads added to the fabric paint enhance the daisy design.

Difficulty Level:
Easy

Materials
* Three shades of denim
* Seam sealant
* Paint applicator (optional)
* Dimensional fabric paint in glossy yellow, blue, turquoise and blue glitter
* Blue and amber mini beads
* Scissors
* Sewing machine
* Tweezers

1 Cut two rectangles 15" x 13¼", each with a flat felled seam 3" from the edge of the 15" side. Cut one piece 12" x 3½" for the bottom of the tote.

2 Cut the following rectangles for the decorative center front patch.
Dark denim 7¾" x 8¼"
Medium denim 6⅞" x 7"
Light denim 5¼" x 5⅜"
Apply seam sealant to edges of each rectangle.

3 Following the manufacturer's directions, paint the daisy design onto the lightest (smallest) rectangle. Use tweezers to add beads to center of daisies. Allow to dry. Add paint to edges of medium and dark rectangles and allow to dry.

4 When paint is dry, stitch small rectangle to medium rectangle, stitch the small/ medium combination to the largest rectangle, and attach to tote front by stitching around the edge of the largest (darkest) rectangle.

5 Place tote front and back right sides together and stitch side seams. Finish with flat felled seams.

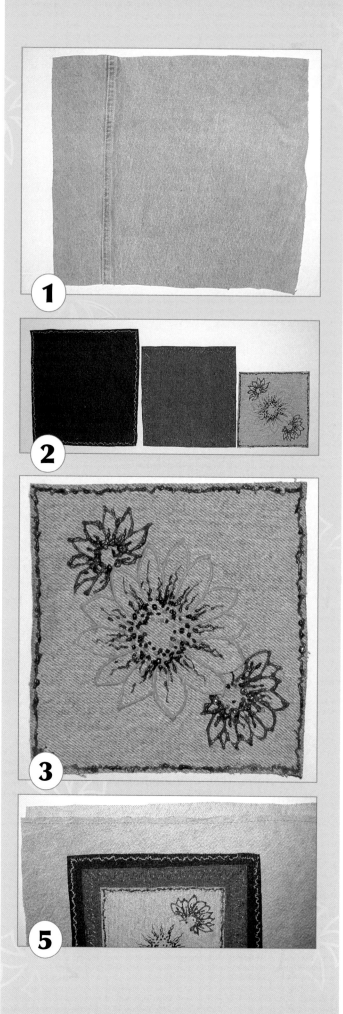

6

6 Turn tote wrong-side-out. Pin bottom section to lower edges of tote, right sides of fabric together. Clip tote seam allowance to stitching line at each corner so you can turn at each corner to continue stitching all around the bottom of the tote. Clip fabric at corners as in photo (clip off the corners of the tote bottom) and zigzag seam edges to finish. Turn right-side-out. Turn seam allowances of purse front and back toward bottom piece and topstitch long edges of tote bottom to better define the edge.

tip
The amount to turn the top edge under depends on the thickness of the denim. If it is really thick it is impossible to turn ¼" and would be more like ⅜". As long as it is even all the way around, it doesn't really matter if it is ¼" or ½".

7 Turn top edge of tote under twice and double stitch the edge.

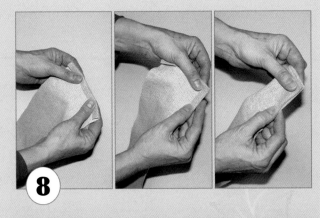

8

8 To make handle, cut denim 4¾" x 38" or as long as desired. Turn all edges of handle under ⅜", fold in half, press, and pin. Stitch ¼" from edge on all sides.

9 Insert end of handles inside bag 1½". Pin in place. Stitch in a square to attach handles to tote.

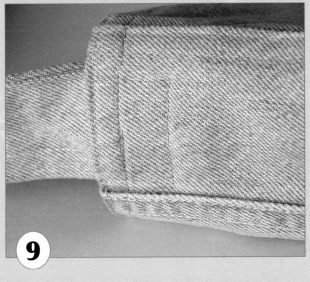

9

Riveted Purse

Here's a unique pouch purse that shows off some more of those jeans labels from your favorite denim brands. The Texas Star rivets are easy to install and can be used with various colors in the center.

1 Use pattern to cut four purse sides. Cut a 10½" circle for purse bottom. Cut interfacing for each piece ½" smaller than pattern and fuse. Cut four diamond shapes from contrasting denim using large diamond pattern. Center jeans labels on large denim diamonds and stitch around labels.

2 Center small diamond pattern in center of each purse side and mark all four points. Connect lines and cut from center of diamond to each point. Fold fabric to inside and pin to form diamond opening. Center label behind opening, pin, and stitch ³/₁₆" outside opening. Repeat on all four sides of purse.

3 Follow manufacturer's instructions to install concho and rivets on each of the four purse sides, with center of conchos 1" away from each side of diamond (2 conchos on each side of purse).

4 Stitch purse sides, right sides together. Finish with reverse flat felled seams.

5 Stitch purse bottom to purse, right sides together. Trim and clip seam.

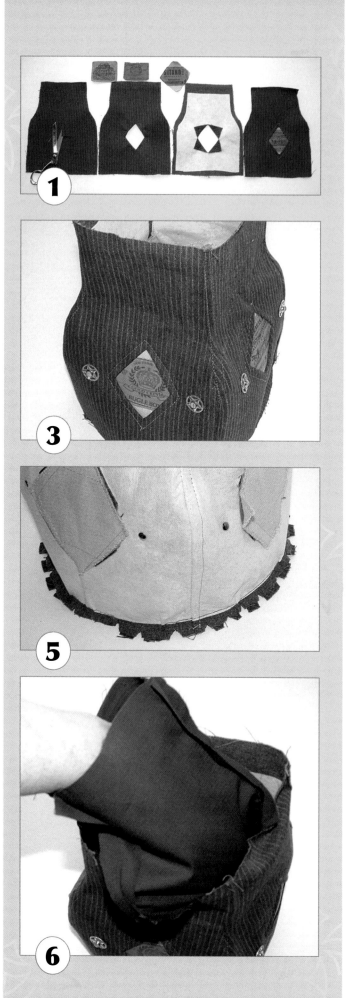

6 Use pattern to cut lining pieces. Cut a 10" circle for the lining bottom. Stitch side pieces together and stitch them to lining bottom using zigzag seam finish on all seams. Turn wrong side of fabric to outside and push lining into purse.

7 Pin lining to purse 1" below top of purse. Turn top edge of purse under 3/16", then turn again to cover raw edge of lining. Stitch 1/4" from edge where lining meets purse inside the purse.

8 To make tabs, cut 8 pieces of denim 3/4" x 3 3/4". Fray edges 3/16" on each side.

9 Turn tab ends under 3/8". Pin tabs to purse top, 1" from each purse side seam. Stitch through all thicknesses, catching ends of tabs on outside and inside.

10 Cut leather lace in half and thread each through four tabs at top of purse. Push leather through drawstring toggle cinches. Tighten to close purse. Tie a knot halfway between end of laces and purse to create handle.

Dangles Purse

This purse's unique design and trendy look make it a great addition to any wardrobe. The contrasting bias tape finish on the edges defines the lines. The bias is fairly easy to apply, with the only challenge being the inside corners of the handle openings.

Difficulty Level: Moderate

Materials

* Light and dark denim

* Iron-on interfacing

* Coordinating, double-fold bias tape (½" folded width)

* Beaded denim trim

* Fabric glue or needle and thread

* Scissors

* Sewing machine

* Thread

* Iron

* Pins

1 Cut four pieces from light denim as indicated on pattern. Also from light denim, cut one 3¾" x 24½" rectangle for the purse sides and bottom. Turn 3¾" ends under twice and topstitch. Find midpoint of rectangle along length and match it, right sides together, to center bottom of lining piece. Stitch. Zigzag over raw edge of bottom/side piece, securing the raw edge to the lining.

2 Repeat stitching bottom/side rectangle to other lining piece.

3 Cut interfacing to fit front and back pieces. Follow manufacturer's instructions to iron interfacing to wrong side of front and back pieces.

4 Zigzag dark denim strip to outside of purse front and back. Use fabric glue to attach trim to edges of dark denim strip, covering denim strip edges. Do not put glue where you will later stitch bias tape to edges of purse (stop about ½" from outer purse edges) or it may gum up your sewing machine needle. You may also hand sew strip to purse.

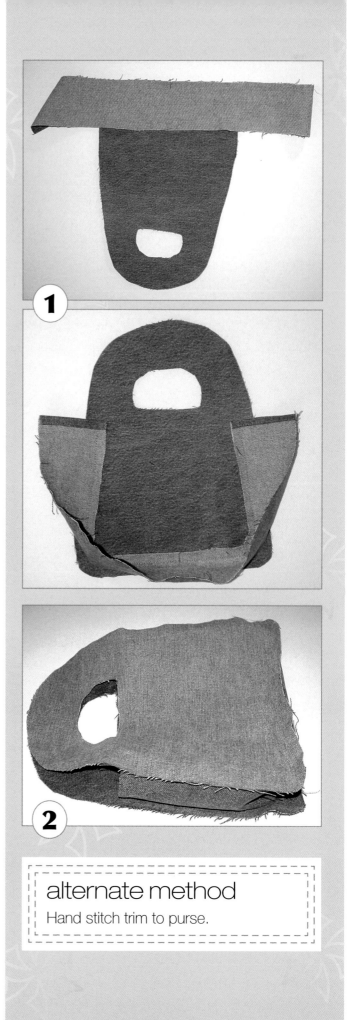

alternate method
Hand stitch trim to purse.

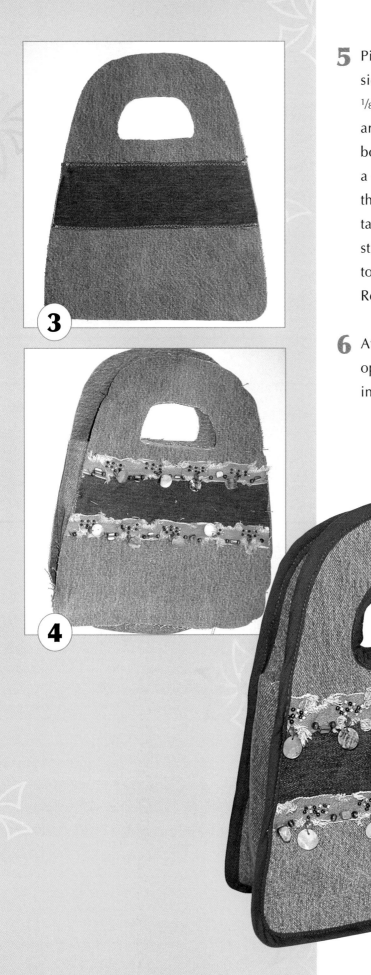

5 Pin baste purse front to lining, wrong sides together. Baste layers together $\frac{1}{8}$" from edges. Trim edges so they are exactly even. Beginning along bottom edge of purse, about 1" from a corner, place bias tape over edge so that it is even on each side. Stitch bias tape around entire edge of purse using straight stitches. Turn end of tape under to finish end, overlapping starting point. Repeat bias on other side of purse.

6 Attach bias tape to cutout handle opening in same manner, easing around inside edges.

Black Purse

Here is a great little purse to match the black vest. It goes together quickly because several elements are taken from the jeans already done—like the zipper top and pockets. The only difficult part is top stitching the last side with the purse already together.

Difficulty Level:
Moderate

Materials
* Black jeans
* 14" hairy gimp
* Two iron-on fashion designs
* 30" lightweight chain
* Scissors
* Sewing machine
* Black thread
* Seam ripper
* Iron
* Press cloth

1 Use pattern to cut front and back pieces with pockets in center of each piece. It is important that the lower point of the pocket is at least ½" from the edge of the pattern. Cut purse top from zipper area of jeans 3¼" x 9½" long. Cut a rectangle 3¼" x 25" long for purse sides and bottom.

2 Cut trim 1" longer than top of pocket. Fold ends of trim under ½" and stitch ends of trim at pocket sides. Stitch long edge of trim along pocket, just through trim and pocket layers, so that the pocket is not stitched closed.

3 Follow manufacturer's directions to attach iron-on fashion design to front of pocket.

4 With right sides together, stitch purse front to long edge of zipper piece. Zigzag seam allowance. Turn seam allowance toward zipper piece and topstitch ¼" from seam line. Repeat with purse back.

5 Remove two belt loops from jeans. Using a seam ripper, open ends of belt loop to make it longer and less bulky so you can stitch it to the purse. Fold in half to make loop. Stitch one loop to each short end of zipper piece, with belt loop ends toward edge of fabric.

tip
Step two may be easier for you if you hand stitch or even use glue.

6 Stitch purse side/bottom piece, right sides together, to purse front, leaving ½" seam allowance at beginning and end. This will later be stitched to the ends of the zipper purse top. Clip corners and point below pocket so the seam will lay flat. Zigzag seam allowance and topstitch, turning seam allowance toward front of purse. Unzip zipper so you can turn the purse right-side-out when finished. Repeat to attach purse back to side/bottom piece.

7 Stitch narrow ends (short ends of zipper purse top) to purse sides. Try not to sew through button closure area, so that you can unbutton it if desired.

8 Turn purse right-side-out. Attach chain handle by opening end links, threading through belt loops, and attaching to seventh link in chain. Try to keep chain from twisting so it will lay flat.

Tan Purse

The handle for this purse, which is made from clear plastic tubing with beads in it, really fits with the beaded trim on the purse. A simpler version could be made by using hook-and-loop tape for the closure and leaving the detail with the buckle off the front of the purse.

Difficulty Level: Experienced

Materials

* Light colored denim

* ½ yd. lightweight fabric for lining

* 10" zipper to match

* 1 yd. beaded trim

* ½ yd. pink ribbon (¹/₁₆")

* 16" clear plastic tubing (½" diameter)

* 4 small gold grommets

* 2 gold binder rings

* Clasp

* Scissors

* Sewing machine

* Thread

* Two silicone scrapers or pieces of smooth, heat-resistant material

* Embossing heat gun

* Hammer

* Grommet setter

1 Cut out purse body and lining pieces and stitch each set with right sides together. Turn purse and lining sections right-side-out. Put lining inside purse. Pin baste pleats in purse (see pattern). Baste along top edge to hold purse and lining edges together. Stitch ribbon edge of trim to purse body.

2 Cut yoke, yoke side, and front belt pieces. Place belt pieces right sides together and stitch along long edges, leaving ends open. Layer seams and notch curved edges. Turn right-side-out. Tuck raw edges at narrow end to inside and topstitch as in photo. Baste wide end of belt to side seam of one front yoke piece.

3 Fold top edge of yoke side pieces under twice and stitch. Pin yoke sides to larger yoke pieces, right sides together. Stitch, forming a circular piece.

4 Place circular yoke piece over purse body, so that the bottom of the yoke overlaps the top edge of the purse body. Fold yoke side pieces in half and tuck to inside of purse.

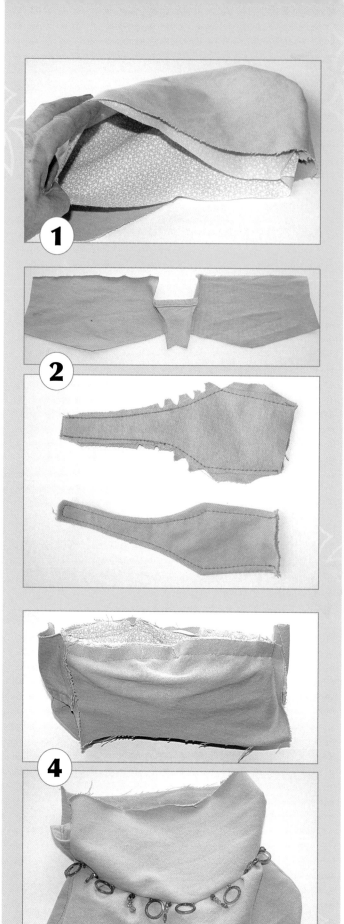

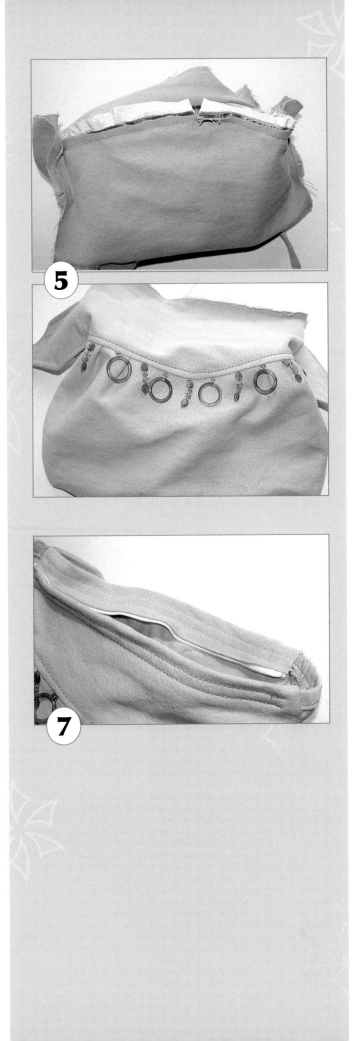

5 Clip center of seam allowance at bottom of V of yoke to stitching line so it will not pucker. Trim yoke/body seam allowance to ¼" wide. Fold lining seam allowance over other seam allowance and topstitch at edge of fold.

6 Fold ends of yoke to inside and pin. Fold the top raw edge of yoke to inside ³⁄₈" and baste. Lay zipper right-side-up with basted edge of yoke on zipper tape, and stitch yoke to zipper. Repeat on opposite side of yoke to attach other side of zipper to yoke.

7 Fold top of yoke down even with side of yoke. Stitch across top of purse ¼" from fold. Stitch again ¼" from that stitching line.

8 Insert ends of front belt pieces through holes in clasp and adjust fabric so clasp is in center of purse. Top stitch, following previous lines of stitching to hold clasps in place. Hand stitching may also be used.

9 To make the handle, string pink beads, removed from the leftover trim, onto $^1/_{16}$" wide ribbon, spacing beads about 1" apart. Let additional ribbon without beads extend out ends of tubing.

10 Carefully heat ends of tubing with heat gun to soften and immediately press between two silicone scrapers or another smooth, heat-resistant material to flatten the ends of the tubing. Follow manufacturer's instructions to install a grommet in each end of the plastic handle, trying to catch the ribbon in the edge of the grommet to hold it in place. Trim ends of ribbon extending beyond end of handle.

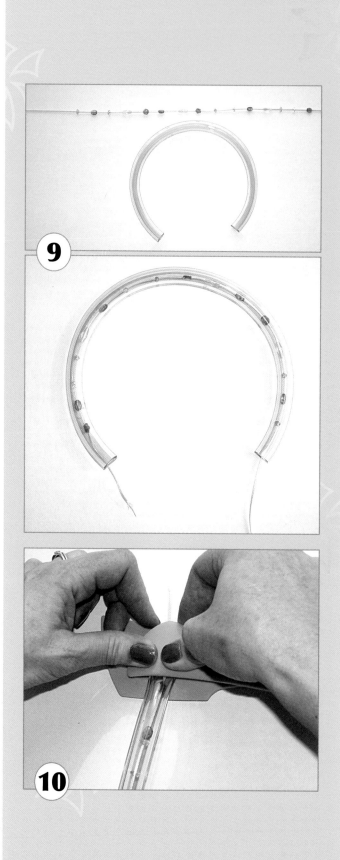

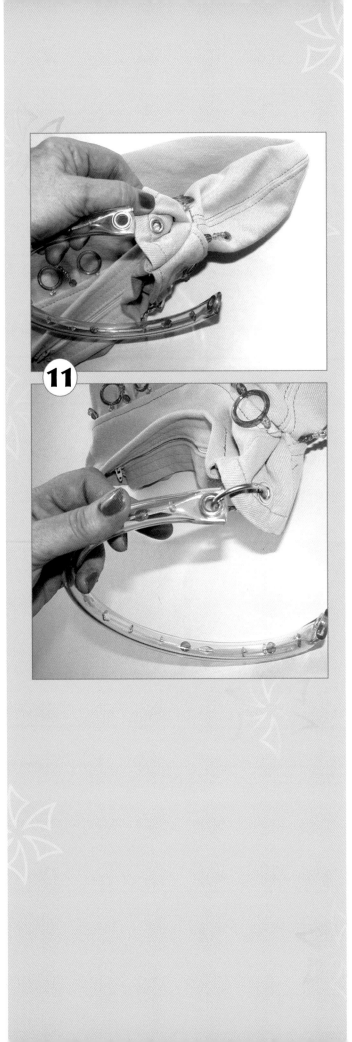

11 Install grommets in center of yoke side pieces. Hook binder ring through grommets in purse and handle to attach handle to purse. Remove to wash purse.

Studded Fringe Purse

This small lined purse has inside pockets and classy metal trim. Select stiffer denim for this purse to give it more natural body.

Difficulty Level: Experienced

Materials:
* Dark and light denim
* Silver button closure from jeans
* Iron-on adhesive (13" x ½")
* 12 metal studs
* Stiff cardboard (3¼" x 10¾")
* Scissors
* Pins
* Sewing machine
* Thread
* Hot glue gun
* Metal stud setter
* Iron

1 Cut pattern pieces from denim for purse and lining, using dark denim for purse flap. Cut trim strip 1" x 13½" wide from thinner denim. Make sure to cut with the straight of the fabric grain so the edge will fray evenly. Remove lengthwise threads along both edges to form fringe. Measure purse flap and cut length of trim to fit, adding ¼" at each end. Turn ends of trim under ¼" and stitch. Apply iron-on adhesive to center back of trim piece. Position trim on purse flap 1" from edge and iron in place.

2 Place purse flap and purse body right sides together and stitch along seam one. Place purse side pieces, right sides down, onto purse body as shown in diagram and stitch, stopping ½" from each end. Clip seam allowance at end of stitching, so you can pivot the side pieces. Trim corners of side pieces only and stitch side pieces to purse body.

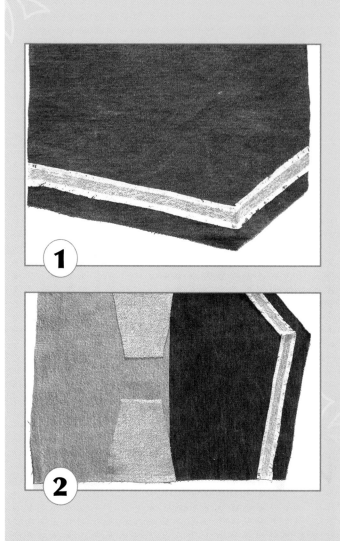

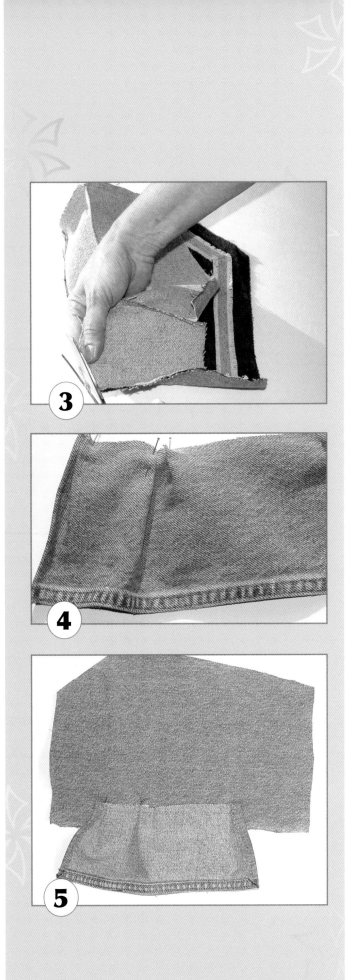

3 Mark dots for stitching line two (see pattern) on wrong side of denim. Fold fabric between dots three and four and stitch ⅛" from fold. This helps define the bottom of the purse. Use hot glue to attach cardboard to bottom of purse unless you will be washing the purse. In that case, use hook-and-loop tape to attach the cardboard or use a piece of stiff plastic.

4 Cut the 4" x 11" inside pocket piece, using a flat felled seam along the 11" edge. Turn the 4" sides under ¼" and stitch to finish edge. Pin baste small pleats at each end and 4" from one end to make a smaller and a larger pocket.

5 Lay unfinished 11" edge of pocket, right sides together, ¾" away from edge two of body lining piece. Stitch seam ½" from pocket edge. Fold pocket up and stitch ends of pocket to lining. Stitch a double line at 4" pleat mark to divide smaller and larger pockets.

6 Assemble lining in same manner as outside of purse. Place lining and purse right sides together, and stitch from side piece, around flap, to other side piece, leaving entire front edge of purse body open. Clip all seams so that the purse edges will lay flat.

7 Cut purse handle 22" x 3¼". Fold ends in ¼". Fold sides in to center of strip. Stitch ⅛" along folded edge only, leaving other edge open (unstitched).

8 Fold handle in half to find center and place stud on center point, fastening through top of handle (one layer) only. Add other studs along handle 2¼" apart from centers of studs until you have placed seven studs.

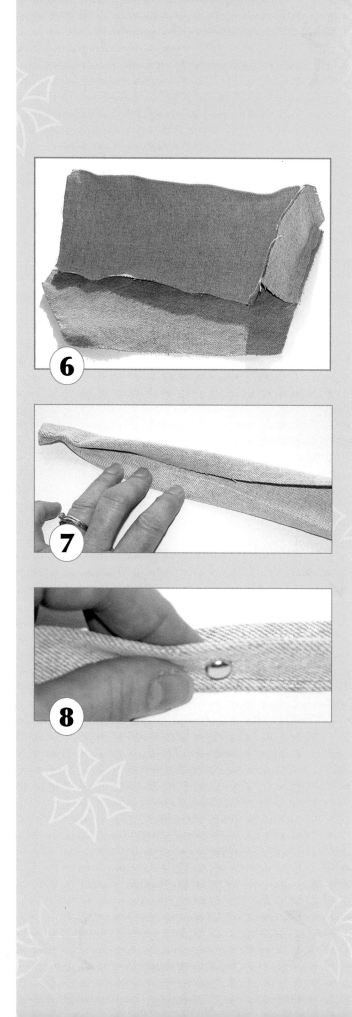

tip

If the handle ends are farther than 1¼" from purse edge, the sewing machine may not be able to stitch to the end of the handle.

9 Use zipper foot and stitch open side of handle ⅛" from edge. Pin handles to center of each purse side, with ends 1¼" from purse edge. Stitch through all layers on each edge of handle. Use hot glue if necessary to hold the end of the handle in place.

10 Cut button area from jeans waistband, leaving 1½" of fabric beyond button. Cut buttonhole area from jeans waistband, leaving 1" of fabric beyond buttonhole. Trim ends as in photo. Trim excess fabric from back of waistband pieces to eliminate bulk. Turn ends to inside and stitch closed. Position buttonhole piece under purse flap so that top of buttonhole is at point of flap. Stitch buttonhole tab to purse front, following topstitching line and also stitching just under fringed trim. Place button into buttonhole and position on front of purse. Pin button tab in place and stitch to front of purse.

Pocket Purse

Here's a cute small purse with a pocket on each side. It's great to grab when you need a few essentials along or just for a fun accessory.

Difficulty Level: Experienced

Materials
* Medium weight denim
* 2 square pockets from jeans
* 3 belt loops from jeans
* Zipper from jeans
* Iron-on interfacing
* 15" beaded eyelash trim
* 12" beaded fringe
* Purse handle with bamboo beads
* Scissors
* Sewing machine
* Masking or painters tape
* Pins
* Seam ripper
* Small needle and thread
* Fabric glue (optional)

1 Cut out pockets as shown leaving ½" jeans fabric around for seam allowances. Clip corners as shown.

2 Cut trim to fit top of pocket, adding ⅜" to each end. Fold ends under. Stitch or glue trim to top edge of pocket, being sure to protect ends so they do not ravel. Cover trim with painters tape so it will not interfere with assembling purse. Repeat with trim on second pocket if desired.

3 Cut strip of denim 3" wide and long enough to go around all four sides of purse. Add ½" seam allowance at both ends of strip. Cut 2" wide piece of interfacing, position in center of denim strip and iron in place following manufacturer's instructions. Lay one pocket piece on side strip with corner of pocket piece ½" from one end of strip, and stitch all edges except top of pocket.

4 Remove zipper from jeans. Tape top of zipper closed so tab will not slide off end. Position zipper on wrong side of strip so closed end of zipper (the one that stays closed when you unzip the zipper) is ½" from top corner of purse.

tip
If using sticky tape, press tape to a piece of fabric several times to make it less tacky.

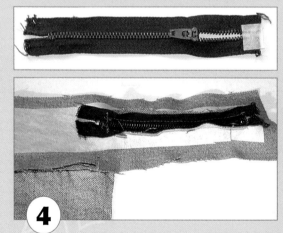

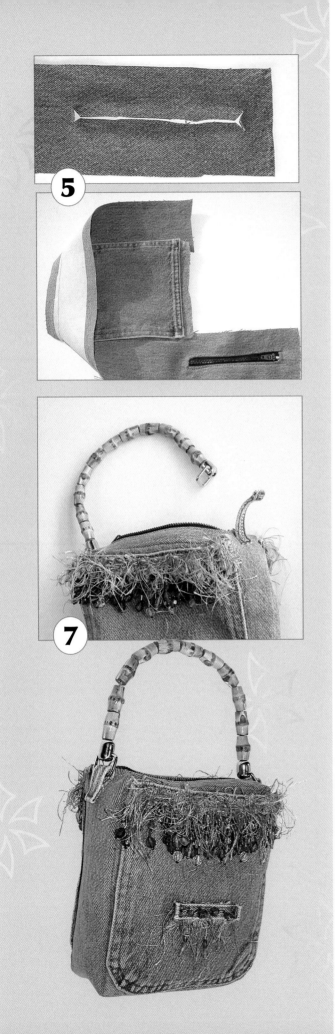

5 Cut a slit in the center of the strip, stopping ¼" before each end of zipper. Cut "Y's" at end of slit. Fold cut area to inside, over zipper. Use zipper foot to stitch around folded area ⅛" from edge. You may want to glue short end tabs of the Y so you don't have to stitch between the zipper cogs, otherwise just stitch carefully between cogs.

6 Stitch top edge of purse fronts to zipper strip on both sides of purse.

7 Use seam ripper to remove stitching at one end of two belt loops. Lay one loop onto purse ¼" beyond end of zipper and stitch in place. Put end of purse handle into loop and glue down other end of loop. Repeat with other side of purse.

8 Thread a small needle and knot end. Poke needle from back to front of third belt loop at one end. Put two or three beads onto needle and push to end of thread. Stitch to hold beads in place. Continue across belt loop and tie off thread on back. Cut eyelash trim to same length as belt loop. Glue trim to back of belt loop and then to side of purse.

Silver Purse

This purse will be the envy of all your friends when they find out that you made it yourself! It's a great shoulder bag with unique embellishments.

Difficulty Level:
Advanced

Materials
* Heavyweight denim
* Silver lamé fabric and cord or silver cording
* 12" blue zipper
* 3 iron-on embroidered appliqués
* Silver jewelry chain
* Sequined flower trim
* Turquoise beads
* Scissors
* Sewing machine
* Hot glue gun
* Jewelry pliers

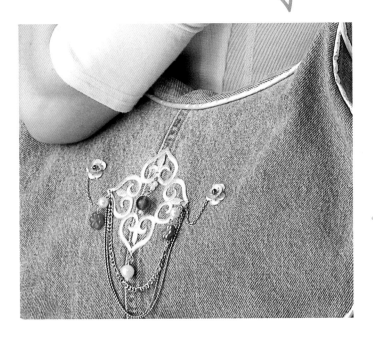

1 Use pattern to cut out pieces of denim with flat felled seams in center of each one.

2 If making cording, cut bias strips of silver lame fabric 1¼" wide. Join seams to make long pieces (see page 9). Fold right-side-out over cord and stitch close to cord using zipper foot.

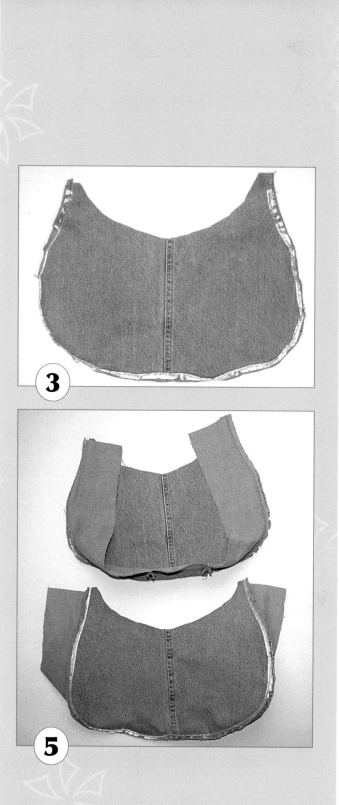

3 Baste cording to edges of purse front and purse back, clipping seam allowance of cording along curved edges. Make sure the raw edge of the cording is along the raw edge of the fabric, not toward the center of the piece.

4 Sew purse side and bottom pieces. Repeat for lining pieces.

5 Stitch purse front to strip with right sides together. Clip seam at curved edges and corners. Stitch lining strip to purse back with right side of lining strip to wrong side of purse back, so lining seam will not show inside purse.

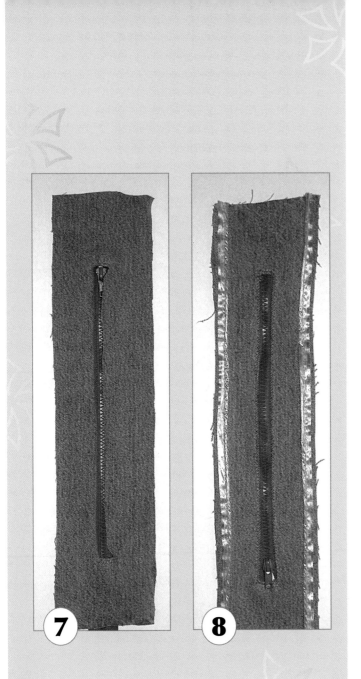

6 Stitch purse back to strip, right sides together, to join outside of purse. Turn purse wrong-side-out. Turn open edge of lining under and topstitch to close. Topstitch other side of strip to match.

7 Compare length of zipper with the length of the slit on the pattern. Center zipper on wrong side of purse top and cut slit at center of zipper to ¼" from each end of zipper. Make a Y slit to end of zipper as in Pocket Purse. Fold all sides of slit to inside and stitch ⅛" from folds.

8 Stitch cording to edges of zipper piece. With right sides together, stitch zipper piece to front of purse. Open zipper. With right sides together, stitch other side of zipper piece to purse back.

9 Stitch through all thicknesses where zipper piece and purse sides meet.

tip

In step nine, you are stitching through all thicknesses—the purse side, side lining, and purse top at the short ends to join it to the purse sides. This seam is on the outside of the purse and will be covered up by the handle where they separate.

10 Sew cording around long part of handle and from dot A to dot B on short piece. Find center of each handle, lengthwise, and lay right sides together (underside of handle will be shorter on each end than outside of handle). Stitch from dot A to opposite dot A, then from B to opposite B. Turn right-side-out.

11 Pin handle to purse. Stitch sides of handle to the point where they must separate. Use hot glue to attach ends of handle to purse.

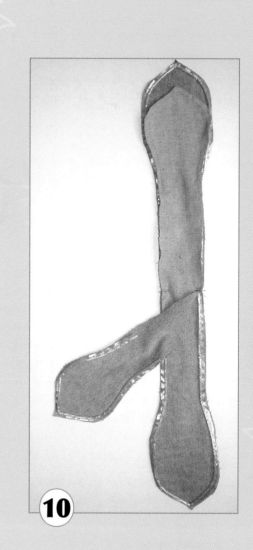

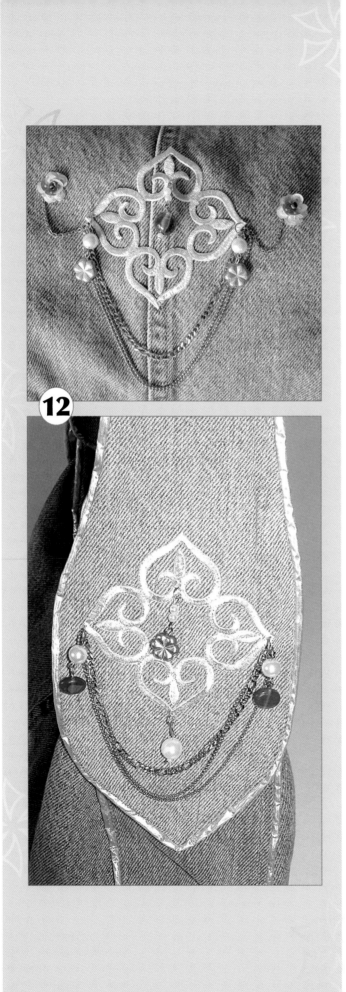

12 Iron appliqués onto front and handles following manufacturer's instructions. Replace beads with colored beads if desired. Add 1½" of jewelry chain to sides of front appliqué. Glue sequin flower over end of chain as shown. Glue bead to center of flower.

Stamped Purse

This purse is simple to construct and has a really classy style. The printed design is stamped with fabric paint. It features a magnetic closure. The cord at the sides is strung through grommets.

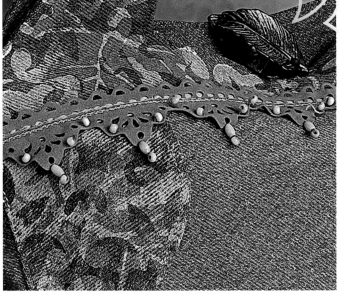

Difficulty Level: Moderate

Materials

* Denim and thread to match
* Extra-wide, double-fold bias tape (tan)
* 12 antique brass grommets (9 mm)
* Fabric paint in buttermilk and burnt sienna
* Fleur-de-lis tile style rubber stamp
* Maple leaf stamp
* Faux suede beaded trim
* 1 yd. heavy braided cord
* Magnetic closure
* Cardboard
* Scissors
* Sewing machine
* Foam brush
* Hammer and grommet setting tools
* Acrylic board
* Needle
* Thread

1 Cut a rectangle from denim with flat felled seam in center lengthwise, 22½" x 15½". Round corners using pattern provided.

2 For inside purse bottom pocket, cut denim 6" x 12". Finish both 6" ends by turning under ¼" and stitching. Turn long sides under ¼" and place in center of oval purse body on wrong side of fabric. Stitch 12" sides, leaving ends open. Cut a piece of cardboard or plastic 4¼" x 11" and slide into pocket. Remove to wash purse.

3 Use pattern to cut four pieces each for patterned patch and purse handles. Apply paint to stamps with foam brush. Stamp all four patch pieces and two handle pieces. Use tile stamp all over and maple leaf stamp over other areas as desired. Allow to dry.

4 Turn curved edge of patch piece under ¼" and stitch. Turn other edges under and pin to purse, lining edge up with piece in bottom of purse. Stitch in place. Repeat with all patch pieces.

5 Beginning at one side, fold bias tape over entire purse edge and stitch very close to edge of tape. Fold end of bias under ¼", overlap starting point, and stitch to finish. Stitch trim over bias tape, making sure not to stretch trim at corners or trim will curl.

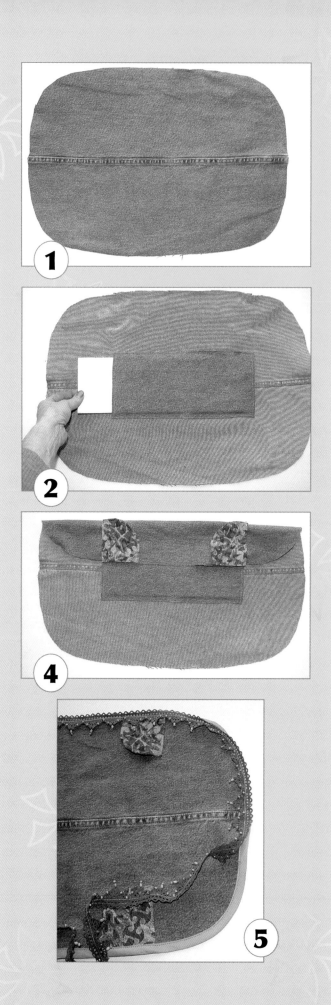

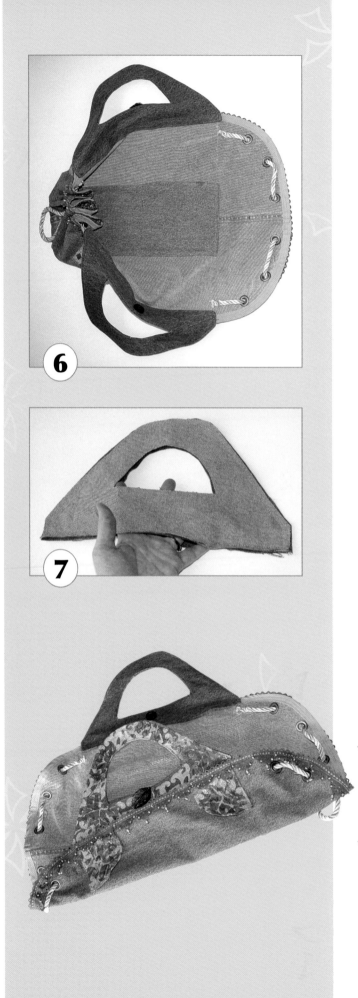

6 Mark grommet placement just under trim using six grommets on each end of purse. Cut holes for center of grommets and install following manufacturer's instructions. String 18" piece of cord through grommets, having ends even with patch on outside of purse. Stitch ends of cord twice about ½" apart to keep cord from raveling and to hold it in place.

7 Place one painted and one plain purse handle right sides together and stitch around outside edge, leaving a 5" opening at the bottom of the handle to turn. Clip curved seam allowance and corners to eliminate bulk. Topstitch all around outer edge, turning 5" opening edges to inside and stitching to close it.

8 Clip corners and curve of inside handle opening. Turn under both seam allowances ¼" to inside. Pin baste or press with iron and topstitch.

9 Pin baste handle to wrong side of purse along top edge, behind bias tape/trim. Stitch through bias tape and handle to attach.

10 Use needle and thread to stitch magnetic leaf closure pieces to purse at lower center of handle piece.

11 Pull cord to gather side of purse and tie knot in cord to hold purse side in place.

Accessories

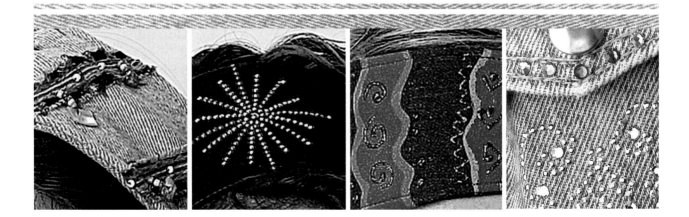

Belt Loop Belt

Turn those belt loops into a belt that's sure to turn heads! It's trendy and no sewing is required. This belt is glued so it's quick and easy to make.

Difficulty Level: Easy

Materials:
* Approximately 38 belt loops that are the same length
* Light blue ribbon ($^3/_{16}$")
* Soft suede trim material (gold)
* 6 yd. soft suede lace ($^5/_{32}$")
* 2 metal buttons with shank back
* Leather glue
* Scissors
* Hot glue gun
* Leather punch
* Hammer
* Needle
* Needle nose pliers

1 Cut belt loops from jeans. Cut several strips of ribbon 2½" long. Lay belt loops, wrong-side-up, as shown in photo. Use hot glue to fasten ribbon to back of belt loops. Continue adding belt loops in pattern until belt is desired length, allowing for leather and ties.

2 Use pattern to cut two suede trim pieces and punch holes in suede as shown. Turn suede to back (wrong-side-up). Push button shanks through holes from right side of suede. Cut two 2" x ¼" strips of suede. Trim one end of each strip to a point and push through button shank, using a needle to start. If strip is too thick, trim it to size of shank opening. Use needle nose pliers to pull strip through both button shanks. Repeat with second piece of suede.

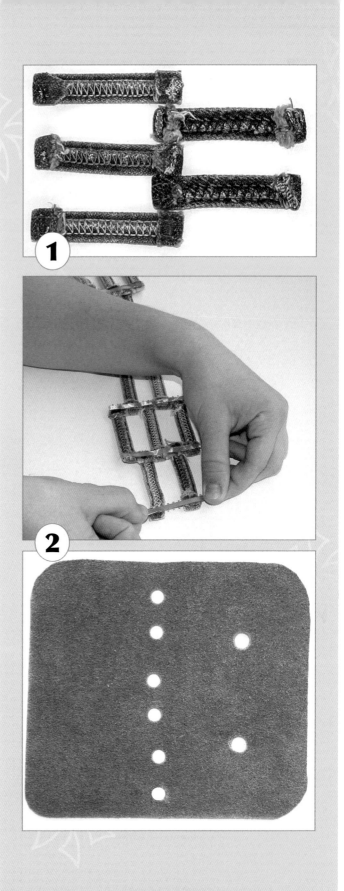

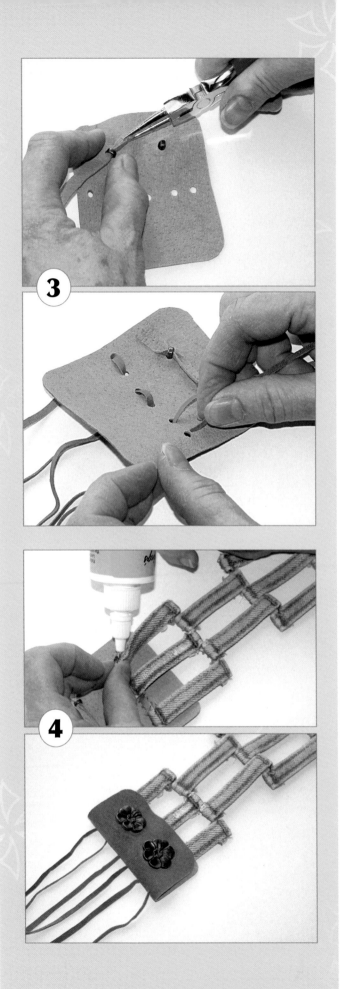

3 Cut suede lace into six one-yard long pieces. Thread one piece (back to front) through the first two holes in the suede trim, pulling ends even. Repeat, using three pieces of lace on each trim piece (six total).

4 Apply leather glue to back of each suede piece and the belt loop ends that will be folded inside the suede piece. Make sure buttons are on front side of belt. Fold suede piece in half over belt loop ends and hold or press until glue is set. Allow to dry completely before wearing belt.

Paisley Belt

This belt is so colorful and fun for someone who needs a little splash of color in her wardrobe. The iron on faux suede is easy to apply. Decorative paint defines the design and the colorful sashes finish it off.

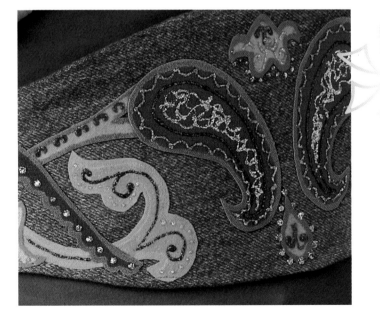

Difficulty Level: Easy

Materials:
* Denim
* Heavyweight iron-on interfacing
* Fusible synthetic suede in hot pink, orange, baby blue
* Fluorescent paint pens in orange, pink, green
* Paint applicator (optional)
* Dimensional fabric paint in silver, blue, and lime
* ⅙ yd. nylon fabric in fluorescent orange
* Scissors
* Sewing machine
* Thread
* Cardboard
* Pins
* Iron
* Press cloth

Rainbow Belt

This colorful belt is very easy to construct and at a low cost, too. You could change the cording to leather lace for another great look.

Difficulty Level: Easy

Materials

❋ Denim

❋ Leather punch size 5 (5 mm or $^{11}/_{64}$")

❋ Blue dimensional fabric paint

❋ Seam sealant

❋ Yellow top stitching thread

❋ 5 yd. rainbow colored cord

❋ Scissors

❋ Sewing machine

❋ Thread

❋ Hammer

❋ Acrylic board

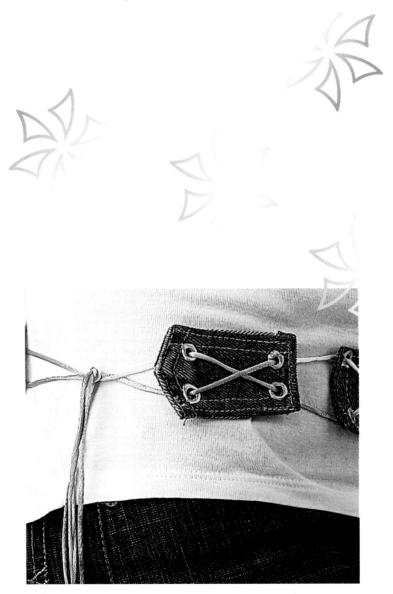

1 For center front of belt, cut around two matching pockets through both pants and pocket. Then cut two pieces each 3¾" long x 2½" wide from tips of the pockets. Open stitching at raw edges just enough to fold in the unstitched sides and end. Trim away any unnecessary fabric in double stitched seam you are opening and tucking in. Topstitch around the piece to match stitching on point.

2 Cut five rectangles 4½" x 2⅝" for other belt pieces. Clip corners. Fold raw edges under ¼" on all edges. Fold fabric wrong sides together, and use double stitching to close.

3 Lay pieces on acrylic board. Use leather punch and hammer to punch holes in each corner trying not to cut through top stitching thread. Seal cut edges with seam sealant. Allow to dry.

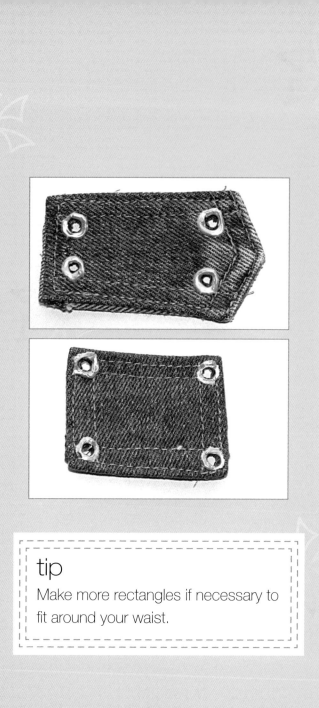

tip
Make more rectangles if necessary to fit around your waist.

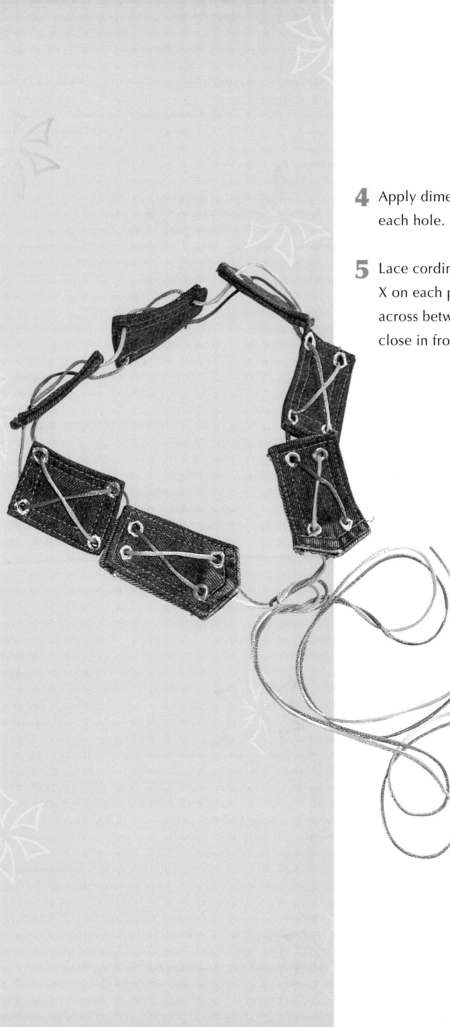

4 Apply dimensional fabric paint around each hole. Let dry.

5 Lace cording through holes with an X on each piece of fabric and straight across between fabric pieces. Tie to close in front.

Ring Belt

This belt is great for a beginning project because it is so simple yet makes a great fashion statement. Try adding an iron-on embellishment in the center of each denim piece for even more sparkle. The finished belt should be approximately 36" long. Add or subtract pieces to adjust length.

Difficulty Level: Easy

Materials
* Dark denim pieces
* 6 metal rings (2")
* 30 pearl studs (size 40)
* Stud setter
* Snap fastener kit
* Scissors
* Sewing machine
* Seam ripper or needle
* Hammer

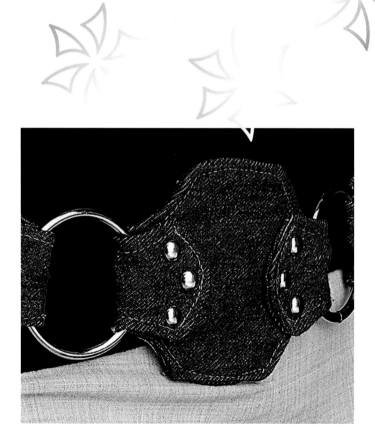

1　Use pattern piece one to cut ten denim pieces. Place two pieces right sides together and stitch from dot A to B, leaving opening to turn right-side-out. Clip seam as shown. Turn right-side-out. Use a knitting needle to push corners out from the inside, or use a seam ripper or knitting needle to pull out from the outside.

2　Fold seam to inside at opening. Topstitch to close opening and add a finished look.

3　Use pattern piece two to cut two denim pieces for belt closure. Put right sides together and stitch from dot A to dot B. Clip curved seams. Turn right-side-out, fold seam in at opening, and topstitch as in step two.

4 Keeping belt pieces flat, arrange pearl studs on tab and push through denim. Use stud setter to attach all studs to all pieces.

5 Follow manufacturer's directions to attach snap fasteners to belt closure piece, making sure that front of snap will be on front of folded piece.

6 To assemble belt, put a ring on first piece and fold tab to the center. Use zipper foot to stitch over previous topstitching to fasten the tab. Continue this process until all tabs and rings are connected. Snap the front closure over front ring. Put belt on and fasten other snap to close belt.

Difficulty Level:
Easy

Materials
* Jeans waistband to
   fit your waist

* Tags from jeans

* Contrasting belt
   loops

* Scissors

* Sewing machine

* Seam ripper

Tags Belt

What a great way to save the tags from all of those favorite jeans! This interesting belt is easy to put together if you have a sharp needle on your sewing machine or tags that are not too thick and leathery. Be sure to select a waistband that fits well as a base.

1 Use seam ripper to remove belt loops from waistband. Open seam at lower edge of waistband to remove it from jeans. Stitch waistband seam closed again.

2 Remove tags from jeans. Remove contrasting color belt loops. Open ends and cut off portion that is folded to the back.

3 Lay tags on waistband with belt loop arranged in "X" fashion and with ends under tags to help with spacing. Use a size 110 Jeans needle to penetrate the thick materials.

4 Stitch tags to waistband placing contrasting belt loops under ends of tags.

Golden Swirls Scarf

Add a little sparkle to your hair with this great scarf. Use lighter weight denim so it's easy to tie and drapes well. Add your favorite beads to the wet paint for extra glam.

Difficulty Level:
Easy

Materials

- Lightweight denim
- Gold self-adhesive beads
- Small glass beads (optional)
- Scissors
- Sewing machine
- Thread
- Pins
- Cardboard

1

1 Cut headband from denim. Turn raw edge of ends under ¼" and stitch. Clip tip end at forty-five degree angle. Fold other raw edges under and stitch.

2 Pin scarf to cardboard before adding self-adhesive beads. Follow manufacturer's instructions to apply self-adhesive beads to scarf in random swirls. Some should appear to be partially off the edge. You may add small glass beads to the wet paint for extra glitz. Allow to dry thoroughly.

note

The white medium of the self-adhesive beads will dry clear, so glass beads will not show up as well when it is dry unless they are a contrasting color.

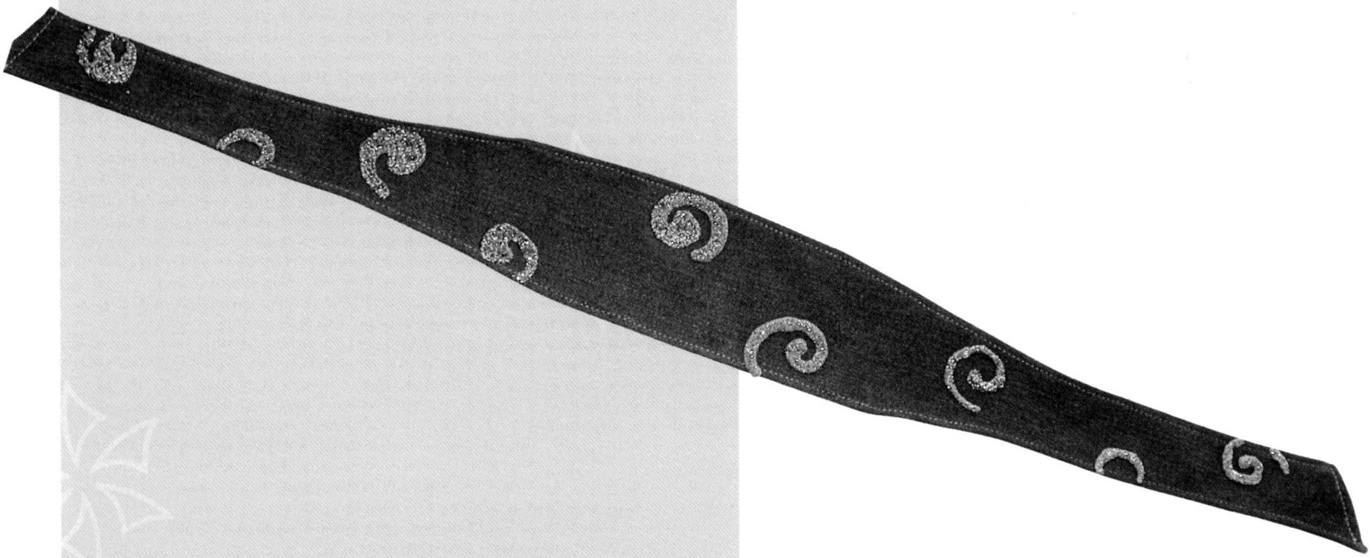

Headbands

Use the basic headband pattern to create these three great looks. Choose either the elastic back style or insert an inexpensive plastic headband. Add an even longer tie and you have yet another option.

Black Elastic Headband

Difficulty Level: Easy

Materials
* Black denim

* Lightweight black fabric for lining

* Black knit for elastic casing

* Heavy iron-on interfacing

* 7" length elastic (3/8")

* Iron-on fashion design

* Scissors

* Sewing machine and thread

* Iron

* Press cloth

* Safety pin

1 Using pattern, cut headband from denim and lining from lighter fabric. Cut interfacing and follow manufacturer's instructions to apply it to back of denim piece. Stitch headband to lining, right sides together, leaving ends open. Layer and clip seam.

2 Turn right-side-out. Position fashion design on center of headband and cut off part that extends beyond edge. Follow manufacturer's instructions to apply fashion design to headband.

3 Cut a 3" x 11" rectangle from knit fabric. Fold fabric in half lengthwise and stitch a ¼" seam along the unfolded edge. Turn right-side-out. Cut elastic 7"–10" long and put a safety pin in one end. Put pin end into tube and slide fabric along pin to pull elastic through tube. Catch end before it goes into tube and stitch tube closed catching elastic. Remove pin and secure elastic at other end of tube.

4 Fold raw edge at end of headband piece to inside and slide end of elastic piece into headband piece. Stitch closed. Repeat at other end.

Wavy Headband

1 Cut headband and lining from denim. Cut interfacing and follow manufacturer's instructions to apply it to back of headband fabric.

2 Trace wavy pattern for colored sections onto suede. Let dry. Cut suede pieces out and follow manufacturer's instructions to fuse to headband.

3 Stitch headband to lining, right sides together, leaving ends open and leaving an opening in the center back about 3" long so you can turn it right-side-out easier. Layer and clip seam. Turn right-side-out. Fold raw edges of opening to inside and top stitch to 1" from ends. This will close the opening and give a crisp edge.

4 Use fabric paint applicator to apply blue glitter paint to headband using photo for suggestions. Allow to dry thoroughly.

5 Cut rectangle 11" x 3" from thinner fabric. Fold right sides of fabric together and stitch raw edges ¼" from edge. Turn right-side-out. Cut elastic 7" long and put a safety pin in one end. Put pin end into tube and slide fabric along pin to pull elastic through tube. Catch end before it goes into tube and stitch tube closed catching elastic. Remove pin and secure elastic at other end of tube.

6 Fold raw edge at end of headband piece to inside and slide end of elastic piece into headband piece. Stitch closed. Repeat at other end.

Difficulty Level: Easy

Materials

* Denim

* Thinner denim fabric for elastic casing

* Heavy iron-on interfacing

* 7" length elastic (³⁄₈")

* Fusible synthetic suede in hot pink, orange, and baby blue

* Fluorescent paint pens in orange, pink, and green

* Dimensional fabric paint in blue

* Fabric paint applicator (optional)

* Scissors

* Sewing machine

* Thread

* Iron

* Press cloth

* Safety pin

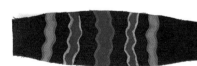

Trimmed Headband

1 Cut headband and lining from denim, adding 1" to each end or enough to cover plastic headband. Cut interfacing and follow manufacturer's instructions to apply it to back of headband.

2 Use zipper foot to stitch trim diagonally to headband.

3 With right sides together, stitch headband to lining, leaving ends open and leaving a 3" long opening in the center along one side so you can turn it right-side-out. Layer and clip seam. Turn right-side-out. Fold raw edges of opening to inside and top stitch around one end and to within 1" from other end.

4 Slide plastic headband into open end. Turn raw edges to inside and stitch closed.

Difficulty Level: Easy

Materials

* Denim

* Lightweight denim fabric for elastic casing

* Heavy iron-on interfacing

* 7" length ⅜" elastic

* ⅔ yd. beaded trim

* Plastic headband

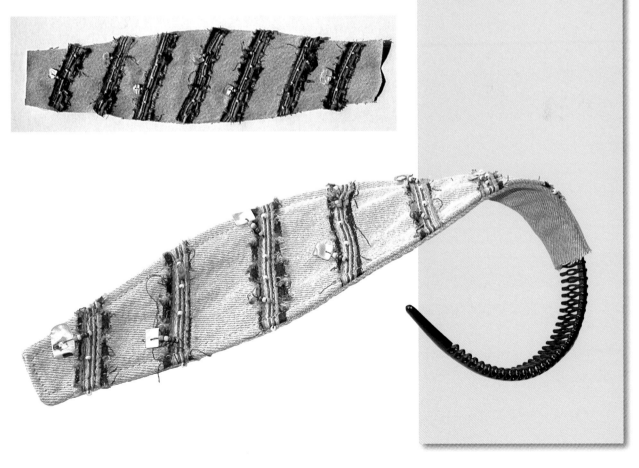

Princess Cell Phone Cover

Here is a way to use one of those cute inside pockets—the ones inside the right front pocket—to make a cover for your cell phone. The embellishments are easy and give it a real girly feel. It can even be put on a narrow belt if you wish.

1 Select a pocket to fit your cell phone, and cut it from the jeans as shown. Remove the waistband, keeping the seam allowance—don't just cut the fabric below the waistband. Rip open the bottom of the pocket. Clip the corners and remove any excess seam allowance from inside the pocket.

2 Cut a piece of the beaded trim ½" longer than the bottom of the pocket. Remove the last beads on the ribbon if necessary so you can turn the ribbon under ¼" on each end. Turn the seam allowance at the bottom of the pocket to the inside and put the ribbon between the seam allowances. Stitch bottom of pocket closed with double stitching.

3 Measure the larger pocket to see that it will work as a flap and then fold around to the back of the holder about two thirds of the way down. This will allow room for a belt to slide through. Cut the sides of the larger pocket to ½" wider on each side than the small pocket. Pin the fabric above the small pocket to the other pocket through one layer only.

4 Open the larger pocket so the inside of it has the small pocket pinned to it. Fold the fabric at the top of the small pocket under ¼" and stitch.

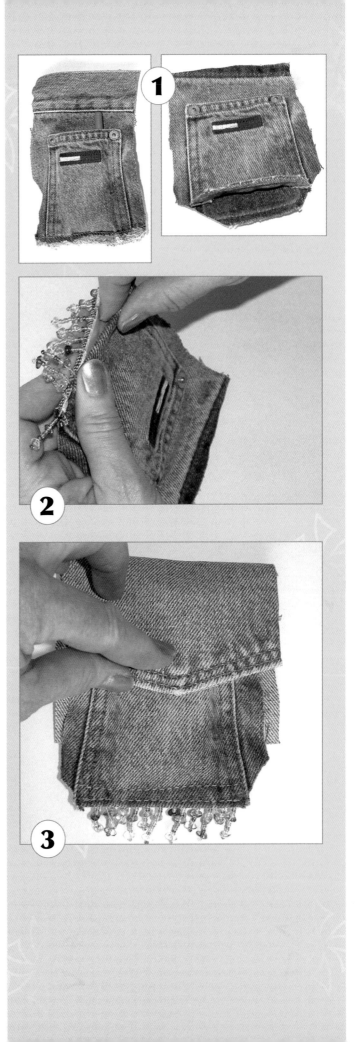

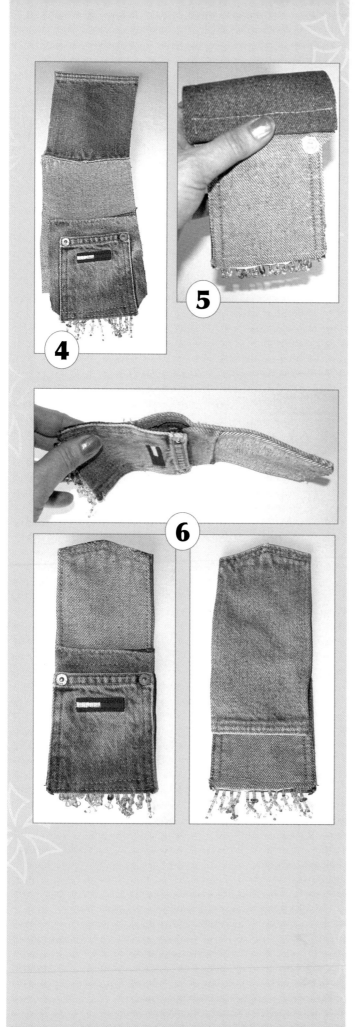

5 Turn the small pocket over to the back. Fold the raw edge of the larger pocket under and stitch at the edge of the fold. Trim the fabric below the stitching line close to the small pocket on both sides.

6 Open topstitching at corners of pointed end of large pocket so you can fold the side edges in and topstitch closed all around flap. Stitch the area that was the "top" of the larger pocket just at the edges to make the opening to put a belt through.

7 Follow manufacturer's instructions to install snap at center of flap.

8 Cut iron-on fashion design just above heart to make two pieces. Follow manufacturer's directions to attach heart half to lower part of small pocket. Attach rest of design above snap-on flap.

9 Use rhinestone applicator to apply hot-fix crystals as shown in photo or as desired.

Resources

VESTS

Black Vest
Expo International Trim #LB5620BK

#IR2504BK
Expo International heart appliqués #SM5951

Dritz Jean-a-ma-jig

JHB Clasp #09053

Lacy Vest
Expo International appliqué #SM5951
Expo International Trim #IR2677BL

DecoArt So Soft Fabric Paints

Dritz Fray Check

Men's Vest
Wright's trim #1861141001 Aztec Braid
Wright's Extra Wide double fold bias tape

Rustic Rebel Iron-On Patch #807039 Tribal Bird/BR

Pant Leg Vest
Delta Stitch Effects Iron-on Transfer Wildflower Border #10 851 0612

Kit Craft BeDazzler Rhinestone Studs
Kit Craft BeDazzler Stud Setter

Rings Vest
Offray Ribbon Trim #164007GG SWT&SOUR YELGR 5
Wright's Deco Discs
Dritz Fray Check

Scalloped Vest
Tulip Slick Fabric Paint
NSI Innovations Fabric Painter
Expo International Trim #IR1886RD

Shawl Collar Vest
Expo International Trim #IR2679
JHB clasp #00902

Sparkles Vest
Tulip Glam-It-Up Iron-On Fashion Design #IRD Design 15 and IRD Design #9
Kandi Corp Hot-Fix Crystals
Kandi Corp Rhinestone Applicator
Expo International Trim #IR2533WH

PURSES

Black Purse
Expo International Trim #LB5620BK
Tulip Glam-It-Up Iron-On Fashion Design™ #IRD Design13

Clutch Purse
Tulip Glitter Fabric Paint

Daisy Tote
Dritz Fray Check
NSI Innovations Fabric Painter
DecoArt So Soft Fabric Paints
Blue Moon Glass Mini Beads

Dangles Purse
Pellon Décor Bond Interfacing
Wright's Wide Double Fold Bias Tape
Expo International trim #IR2673BL

Pocket Purse
Pellon Décor Bond Interfacing
Expo International Eye Lash Trim #SM3664BG
Hirshcberg Schultz & Co. beaded trim #TCK1111-123

Riveted Purse
Pellon Décor Bond Interfacing
Tandy Leather Factory Bezel Concho Rope Edge Star
Tandy Leather Factory Turquoise Rivets 7 mm
Tandy Leather Factory Decorative Rivet Setting Kit

Silver Purse
Hirschberg Schulz Chic Boutique silver flower Trim #MSI #1321736
Hobby Lobby Stitch Art embroidered heart appliqué

Stamped Purse (Painted Purse)
Wright's Wide Double Fold Bias Tape – Spice
DecoArt So Soft Fabric Paints
Rubber Stampede Wrought Iron Stamp
American Traditional Stencil Maple Leaf Stamp
Expo International Trim #IR2561
JHB Magnetic Leaf Closure

Studded Fringe Purse (Purse 1)
Therm O Web HeatnBond Ultrahold
Kit Kraft BeDazzler Pearl Studs size #40
Kit Craft BeDazzler Stud Setter

Tan Purse (Touch of Pink Purse)
Expo International Trim #IR3780FS
Offray 1/16" ribbon
JHB clasp #009360

BELTS & ACCESSORIES

Belt Loop Belt
Tandy Leather Factory Velvet Suede Trim Piece – Gold
Tandy Leather Factory Velvet Suede Lace – Gold
Tandy Leather Factory Leathercraft Cement

Paisley Belt
Kandi Corp Zwade Fusible Synthetic Suede
Krylon Brights Fluorescent Paint Pens
NSI Innovations The Ultimate Fabric Painter
Tulip Glitter Fabric Paint – Silver, Blue, Lime

Rainbow Belt
Tandy Leather Factory Mini Punch
Set
Dritz Fray Check
Trimtex Variegated Rattail ribbon

Ring Belt
Kit Kraft BeDazzler Pearl Studs size
#40
Kit Craft BeDazzler Stud Setter

Tags Belt
(None)

Princess Cell Phone Cover
Expo International beaded Trim
#IR1896WHM
Tulip Glam-It-Up Iron-On Fashion
Design #IRD Design1
Kandi Corp Hot-Fix Crystals
Kandi Corp Rhinestone Applicator

Headbands
Black Elastic Headband
Pellon Décor Bond Interfacing
Tulip Glam-It-Up Iron-On Fashion
Design Star Burst

Wavy Headband
Pellon Décor Bond Interfacing
Kandi Corp Zwade Fusible Synthetic
Suede
Krylon Brights Fluorescent Paint
Pens
NSI Innovations The Ultimate Fabric
Painter
Tulip Glitter Fabric Paint - Blue,

Trimmed Headband
Pellon Décor Bond Interfacing
Expo International beaded Trim
#IR2678BL

Golden Swirls Scarf
DecoArt Fashion beadz Bead Writer
- Gold

American Traditional Designs
442 First NH Tpke.
Northwood, NH 03261
Phone: 1-800-448-6656
www.americantraditional.com

Blue Moon Beads
7855 Hayvenhurst Avenue
Van Nuys, CA 91406
www.bluemoonbeads.com

DecoArt, Inc.
P.O. Box 386
Stanford, KY 40484
www.decoart.com

Delta Technical Coatings/Rubber
Stampede
www.deltacrafts.com

Expo International
Houston, TX 77036
www.expointl.com

Dritz
Prym-Dritz Corporation
Spartanburg, SC 29304
www.dritz.com

Delta Technical Coatings/Rubber
Stampede
Whittier, CA 90601
www.deltacrafts.com

Hirshcberg Schultz & Co.
Warren, NJ

JHB International, Inc.
1955 South Quince St
Denver, CO 80231
www.buttons.com

Kandi Corp
PO Box 8345
Clearwater, FL 33758
www.kandicorp.com

Kit Kraft
12106 Ventura PL
Studio City, CA
www.kitkraft.biz

Krylon Products Group
Cleveland, OH 44115
www.krylon.com

NSI Innovations
105 Price Parkway
Farmingdale, NY 11735
www.nsiinnovations.com

Offray
Berwick Offray LLC
2015 West Front Street
PO BOX 428
Berwick, PA 18603-0428
www.offray.com

Pellon
Freudenberg Nonwovens
Pellon Consumer Products Division
4720-A Stone Drive
Tucker, GA 30084
www.pellonideas.com

Rustic Rebel and Stitch Art
Hobby Lobby

Revamp Your Wardrobe
with Alteration Inspiration

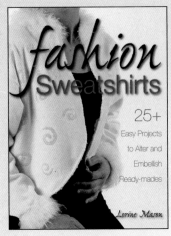

Fashion Sweatshirts

25+ Easy Projects to Alter and Embellish Ready-mades

by Lorine Mason

Features 29 ready-made sweatshirt transformations for women and children, using sewing, embroidery, knitting and crocheting techniques, while incorporating embellishments such as buttons, fringes, lace, appliqué, iron-ons and beads. Easy, fun and inexpensive.

Softcover • 8-¼ x 10-7/8 • 128 pages
75 color photos, plus 25 illus. & charts
Item# FSHSW • $22.99

AlterNation

Transform, Embellish, Customize

by Shannon Okey
and Alexandra Underhill

This is the indie-crafters DIY fashion guide to personalizing wardrobes with a wide range of no-sew and low-sew techniques.

Softcover • 8 x 10 • 144 pages
250 color illus. & 10 bw illus.
Item# Z0713 • $19.99

Altered Style

Sewing & Embellishing Wearable Fashions

by Stephanie Kimura

Learn how to create new garments and goodies by altering items you already own. Transform a worn pair of jeans into a skirt or a bag, and open a whole new world of wardrobe opportunities

Softcover • 8-1/4 x 10-7/8 • 128 pages
200+ color photos
Item# Z1658 • $22.99

Transforming Fabric

30 Creative Ways to Paint, Dye, and Pattern Cloth

by Carolyn A. Dahl

Discover the secrets of dyeing, painting and patterning beautiful cloth with this inspiring guide. Explore details about general techniques plus, lots of fresh ideas to ensure successful results.

Softcover • 8-¼ x 10-7/8 • 160 pages
200 color photos, plus illus
Item# TSFF • $23.99

Low-Sew Boutique

25 Quick & Clever Projects Using Ready-Mades

by Cheryl Weiderspahn

Transform common place mats, towels, pot holders and rugs into 25+ innovative fashion accessories, such as a backpack, eyeglass case, purse and more, by following the detailed instructions and 175 color photos and illustrations in this unique guide.

Softcover • 8-¼ x 10-7/8 • 128 pages
175 color photos
Item# Z0378 • $22.99